S0-CNH-239

LITTLE ROCK
ONE FROM THE HEART

By Bill Worthen

Photo Editing by Matt Bradley

Profiles in Excellence by Kelley Bass

Captions by Jim Morgan

Art Direction by Anne Castrodale

URBAN
TAPESTRY
SERIES

TOWERY
PUBLISHING, INC.

TOWERY PUBLISHING, INC.

▲ BRETT LILE

Interstate 430, which skirts the city to the west, was obviously planned by someone with a sense of drama. That's the Arkansas River peeking through the chiseled bluffs.

PAGES 2 AND 3: BILL PARSONS

Library of Congress Cataloging-in-Publication Data

Worthen, William B., 1947-
     Little Rock : one from the heart / by Bill Worthen and Matt Bradley. Profiles in excellence / by Kelley Bass.
          p. cm. -- (Urban tapestry series)
     Includes index.
     ISBN 1-881096-29-7 (alk. paper)
     1. Little Rock (Ark.)--Civilization.   2. Little Rock (Ark.)--Pictorial works.   3. Business enterprises--Arkansas--Little Rock.
I. Bradley, Matt, 1947-   . II. Bass, Kelley, 1959-   Profiles in excellence.   III. Title.   IV. Title: Profiles in excellence.
V. Series.
F419.L7W835   1996   96-34244
976.7'73--DC20   CIP

Copyright © 1996 by Towery Publishing, Inc.

All rights reserved. No part of this work may be reproduced or copied in any form or by any means, except for brief excerpts in conjunction with book reviews, without prior written permission of the publisher.

Towery Publishing, Inc., 1835 Union Avenue, Memphis, TN 38104

Publisher: J. Robert Towery
Executive Publisher: Jenny McDowell
National Sales Manager: Stephen Hung
National Marketing Director: Eleanor D. Carey
Marketing Coordinator: Carol Culpepper
Project Directors: Chad Kauffman, Robert Philips, Rick Teague

Executive Editor: David B. Dawson
Senior Editor: Michael C. James
Profiles Manager/Associate Editor: Lynn Conlee
Associate Editors: Mary Jane Adams, Lori Bond, Carlisle Hacker

Technical Director: William H. Towery
Production Manager: Brenda Pattat
Production Assistant: Jeff McDonald

$\mathcal{C}$ONTENTS

MATT BRADLEY

THE ACCURATE PICTURE OF LITTLE ROCK TODAY IS BLURRED. OH, THERE ARE PLENTY OF DETAILS—FACES AND FEET, CLOTHES AND CARS, HOMES AND OFFICES—BUT THEY ARE OBSCURED BY THE PUSH AND PULL OF IDEAS, THE SHUFFLE OF PLANS, THE FACT OF BECOMING. LITTLE ROCK IS AS MUCH IN PROCESS TODAY AS IT HAS BEEN AT ANY TIME IN ITS EXISTENCE. AND, INSTEAD OF WORRYING ABOUT a Yankee invasion, as in mid-1863, or even awaiting the national election of 1992, this movement comes from within. Don't get me wrong: Our step might not be as firm as we would like. But this is a pretty rich and exciting time in our history, and if our collective heart can be the ultimate guide, this might be our best defining moment so far.

I thought Little Rock's high point might have come in 1992. After all, one of us was being elected to the presidency of the United States of America, the most important and powerful job in the world. Bill was one of us. He was a neighbor, perhaps the most neighborly governor in recent memory—jogging around our streets, often having eluded the security staff; with Hillary and Chelsea, making the governor's house a home full of activity and liveliness; and enjoying a kid-centered life in Little Rock. Sure, most of us had seen a wart or two, but that made his election that much more wonderful for us—the guy shared our humanity. Shoot, there were times when he really did share our pain!

WESLEY HITT

For me, there has been no more vibrant a moment of civic pride than when we watched Bill Clinton's acceptance of the presidency in front of our old State House. This Arkansas boy, who'd come to find fame and fortune in the big city, was standing before Arkansas' greatest symbol of intent and promise, affirmed by the nation as its leader. But was this our city's defining moment? No, that would be too easy.

Of course, for many people, Little Rock's defining moment is more personal. We don't live somewhere because of great civic occurrences; we are here for the day-to-day life. And we look to the city to give us the opportunity for our own defining moments. These moments appear in grand occasions or in quiet relations—at a monumental fireworks display at Riverfront Park, during a discreet but remarkable liaison on the road to some not-quite-developed subdivision, on the dance floor at Juanita's, at a school honors assembly, in church, and at places in between. We're human, after all, and memories and significance attach themselves through personal experience. Little Rock, then, is a personal place where one hopes, dreams, struggles, resolves, and keeps on.

In 1956 President Eisenhower signed the interstate highway bill, which changed the face of American cities everywhere. Between the early 1960s and late 1970s, Little Rock was almost always building a loop or a link or a bridge or a bypass. This view looks from the southeast corner of the city, where I-30 connects with I-630 (OPPOSITE).

More and more, sundown means heading home to the suburbs, sometimes via these loops around the city. But recently, downtown forces have launched an ambitious riverfront development in hopes of luring people back into the city.

PAGES 6 AND 7: BILL PARSONS

OUR FAIR CITY CARRIES A PUBLIC PERSONA TOO. WHILE I'D LOVE TO LIVE UP TO OUR COMMUNITY'S IMAGE, I SOMETIMES FEEL WE MUST LIVE IT DOWN, OR AT LEAST EXPLAIN THE HECK OUT OF IT. I SUPPOSE THERE'S NO USE COMPLAINING; SELF-PITY IS THE LEAST ATTRACTIVE OF THE INDUL-gences, and every positive image contains within it the seed of its opposite. It's a yin-yang thing. But darned if we haven't been yanged real hard right on the heels of our yins.

MATT BRADLEY

Our two most newsworthy examples: Central High School and Bill Clinton.

In 1956 Little Rock shone as a moderate and humane southern city where the new law of the land—equal educational opportunity for all races as defined by the Supreme Court—could be safely applied. Right? Wrong. In 1957 the Central High crisis splattered our name all over the world as a symbol of race division and backwardness. It was as if something in the city had suddenly died. Maybe it was innocence, maybe self-delusion. Maybe it was just that Central High was the ugliest event in Little Rock since the city's last lynching in 1927, a bare 30 years earlier.

From that perspective—with the continued occasional killing of African-Americans in other parts of the South—the courage of the Little Rock Nine and their parents and supporters, especially Daisy Bates, was astounding. These people chose to apply the law of the land in the *Brown v. Board of Education* ruling by taking the 'point position' for integrating the Little Rock schools. Even in this moderate Southern city, what consequences would come of the "blackening" of Central High, the symbol of great white high school education in the state?

BILL PARSONS

Maybe it's the galvanizing influence of watching our fellow Arkansans get beat up in Washington, but today Little Rock seems more unified than ever.

A big thruway in Little Rock is Capitol Avenue, with its namesake at the far end. The large bank buildings along this route prompt some wags to call the street "capital" avenue.

The scene at Central High—the troops, the mobs, the Nine—flashed around the world, as the new medium of television flexed its network news muscles. This was the first civil rights battle to enter the nation's homes, and Little Rock became a symbol.

The crisis progressed through 1957-1958 as National Guardsmen first resisted and then, on Dwight Eisenhower's belated order, enforced integration at Central. It lingered through the "lost" year of closed high schools only to be resolved, finally, in 1959 when the city's voters replaced three segregationist school board members in a heart-poundingly dra-matic election, after the board's attempt to purge integrationist school district employees. Among the heroes of the crisis at Central High, besides the nine children who put their lives on the line, were the Women's Emergency Committee to Open Our Schools and the Stop This Outrageous Purge (STOP) groups. Founder of the Women's Emergency Commit-tee Adolphine Fletcher Terry, one of the most remarkable people of this or any city, made a now famous remark, "I see the men have failed again. I'll have to send for the women." Those years pulsed with primary emotions, and so many folks, for better or worse, showed us what they were made of.

◀ MATT BRADLEY

On the other hand, the 1950s were a defining time in Little Rock's history. The region received a monumental boost from the federal government when the Little Rock Air Force Base landed in Jacksonville. (It was only a few years later that we learned that the blessings of increased commerce, higher visibility, and federal money came with an interesting downside: We ranked high enough to have our name on a Russian ICBM missile.) In addition, construction began on another huge federal project, the McClellan-Kerr Arkansas River Navigation System. And civic leaders moved to create an industrial park so this nice southern town could attract manufacturing jobs from the rusting North.

▲ MATT BRADLEY

The pressures of the automobile culture (and maybe a touch of white flight) began to drive the community out from its heart to the west. The junior college became Little Rock University out on old Hayes Street (soon to be University Avenue), while the Village Shopping Center sprouted a little further south at Asher. The Village was the first of those suburban retail centers—followed by Park Plaza and University Mall—that quickened the decline of downtown as *the* place to shop. Thus began the end of a tradition stretching back to the early days of the last century.

So, the 1950s was a decade of progress punctuated by an amazing episode that touched everyone in Little Rock and that reminded us of the racial gulf and the lack of leadership in the community. Still, those were progressive times and the city felt that its problems lay beyond even politics and constituencies. Another of those positive-negative things.

Everybody thinks they know all there is to know about Little Rock's Central High School (ABOVE). What most don't realize is that when it opened in 1927, it was the largest high school in the nation—a distinction it held until the 1940s. It was also labeled "America's Most Beautiful High School" by the National Association of Architects.

Politicians have a completely different measure of beauty. You can gauge the date of Bill Clinton photos by checking his hair color. Sure enough, this is Governor Clinton, circa 1992, campaigning for the job that would end his gubernatorial streak at 12 years (OPPOSITE).

*I*F YOU'RE TOO YOUNG TO REMEMBER THAT YIN YANG, HOW ABOUT 1992, WHEN NATIVE SON BILL CLINTON ASCENDED TO THE HIGHEST OFFICE IN THE LAND? HE FOUND HIMSELF (AS HE DOES TODAY) HOUNDED AND TORMENTED FOR ANY NUMBER OF SINS—GRAND AND PETTY, VAGUE AND ELUSIVE. THE FACT THAT IT happened to our boy was bad enough, but the national press and the political opposition, aided and abetted by some misguided locals, smeared the place as well as the man.

So, to live in Little Rock is to carry wisdom of the duality of life—life and death, rich and poor, male and female, the Trojans and the Razorbacks, Granite Mountain and Chenal Valley, Geyer Springs and Rodney Parham, Fourche Bottoms and Pinnacle Mountain, "Speak Up for Decency" and "Speak Up for Liberty." Little Rock accepts these dualities. It's been that way for a long time.

Our "little rock" is a prime example. The story goes that travelers from New Orleans, heading north by way of the mighty Mississippi and then west on the Arkansas, could travel all the way to our little outcropping, where the foothills of the Ouachita Mountains dip their toes in the passing stream, without seeing a single rock. Did we honor this rock's notable presence? No, we whacked off part of it instead, and built a railroad bridge on what remained. But we've come around again: Today Riverfront Park celebrates the presence of our geological namesake, and rock groups and symphony orchestras regularly serenade it.

▲ WESLEY HITT

Cities are living archaeology: The Metrocentre Mall, created in 1978, dates back to the period when everybody thought closing streets and turning them into pedestrian walkways was the key to vital downtowns (ABOVE). Some of the mall has since been reopened to vehicular traffic, but a portion of it remains as a pleasant oasis for workers to catch a few rays during a lazy lunch hour or pick up a little something for the boss if they've lingered too long (RIGHT).

In 1821 the General Assembly declared these foothills to be the territorial capital. The seat of government was thereby spared the flood and miasma that plagued the old colonial remnant called Arkansas Post. The post, having lost its only asset when it lost the government, died a lingering death until it was resurrected by another government entity, the National Park Service.

The presence of state government makes Little Rock the backdrop for rich and varied drama. The General Assembly has always been another of those mixed blessings, yin and yang, serving up everything from tragedy to farce over a period of some 160 years.

▲ BILL PARSONS

Perhaps the most notorious event associated with the legislature occurred in 1837, just one year after Arkansas achieved statehood. Our new state—flushed with the pride of equality with the 24 older ones—had a brand-new State House in which to practice democracy. Given Arkansas' lean experience, you can understand how some of us might not have grasped the idea of the rule of law over that of men.

While attending to the business of Arkansas, Speaker John Wilson, from his lofty platform in the House chamber, detected some razzing from Representative J.J. Anthony. Wilson's knife proved quicker than his brain, and Anthony died on the point of order, in a pool of blood on the floor of the House. Ever ready to find fault, commentators labeled the incident a breach of legislative protocol, and we were set

WESLEY HITT

upon with all sorts of criticisms. "Arkansas is the head-quarters of Bowieism, and Little Rock, the centre from whence the 'code of honour' radiates over the province," one English journalist editorialized. Charles Dickens noted that "stabbings in the legislative halls" were a logical by-product of slavery in the South. This event did for Arkansas in the 19th century what the Central High crisis did in the 20th: It gave us an image we could have done without. In 1889, more than 50 years after Antony's demise, Frederick Douglass visited Little Rock and evoked the killing in a newspaper interview, saying, "The evil repute cast abroad by that event yet clings around the fair name of your state."

BILL PARSONS

There's no way to skirt the subject— there's a whole lot of money in Little Rock, much of it associated with the Stephens family, for whom this gleaming new skyscraper was named (ABOVE). For years, Stephens, Inc. was the largest investment bank located off Wall Street. It was also Stephens that helped Sam Walton take his little company, Wal-Mart, public. Speaking of money, one of the city's finest shopping districts is the elegant Pulaski Heights, a mile from downtown (LEFT).

We can visit the exact site of this confrontation. The old State House rests with a commanding view of the Arkansas River, just as it did before the territory advanced to statehood. In a grand and visionary act for early Little Rock, territorial governor John Pope decided to create a formidable symbol of the democracy the state would be taking on in 1836. The State House was quickly labeled Pope's Folly, but the large Greek temple on the Arkansas frontier, with massive porticos facing the river on one side and the community on the other, had to give the population pause. The Greek style proved popular in the South for the evocation of the philosophical seat of democracy and for the justification of another ancient practice, the institution of slavery. The magnificent building, therefore, could send a mixed message, depending on one's place in society.

BILL PARSONS

MATT BRADLEY

OTHER REMARKABLE THINGS OCCURRED AT THE STATE HOUSE. AT TWO SECESSION CONVENTIONS IN 1861, THE DELEGATES ELECTED FIRST TO STAY WITH THE UNITED STATES AND THEN, AFTER FIGHTING BEGAN AT FORT SUMTER, TO SECEDE. ONLY ISAAC MURPHY HELD FAST FOR THE Union in the final vote. A bouquet of flowers was dramatically dropped from the balcony honoring Murphy's allegiance to the United States. This war they were getting into would mark us all.

At first, the city showed grace and civility. Even before secession, occupation of the United States Army Arsenal in Little Rock became a bone of contention between southern hotbloods and the federal authorities. Captain James Totten wisely and gallantly relinquished his post at the arsenal to federal authorities rather than risk a confrontation that might precipitate a larger conflict. His action was so appreciated by the women of Little Rock that they presented Totten with a sword. The arsenal's Tower Building—which had

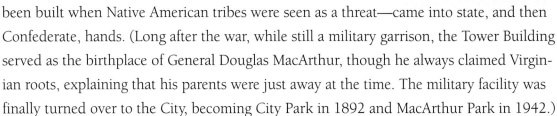

been built when Native American tribes were seen as a threat—came into state, and then Confederate, hands. (Long after the war, while still a military garrison, the Tower Building served as the birthplace of General Douglas MacArthur, though he always claimed Virginian roots, explaining that his parents were just away at the time. The military facility was finally turned over to the City, becoming City Park in 1892 and MacArthur Park in 1942.)

Little Rock coped with the Civil War fairly well. First, most citizens loyally supported the southern cause, mustering troops for both service in the East and defense of home. But the city was hard to defend, and when Union troops came calling, we hardly put up a skirmish. The saddest commentary on the defense of Little Rock came when Confederate Generals John Marmaduke and Marsh Walker found more importance in fighting each other than in engaging the enemy.

Aside from a few ugly episodes, the Union forces treated the city with some respect. The humiliation of pioneer editor and real estate mogul William E. Woodruff did not endear the Federals to the local population, nor did the hanging of David Owen Dodd, a spy who became known as the "boy martyr of the Confederacy." Dodd was held at the Ten-Mile House, hanged in MacArthur Park, and buried with all sorts of luminaries in Mount Holly Cemetery.

But the Civil War has persisted in our consciousness for generations. When my Aunt Jane spoke of "the War," you knew it was not the Great War, or the Second World War, or Korea, or the war of my youth, Vietnam—all wars through which she lived. It was the War between the States, which, because of her upbringing, lived through her. This was the only defeat that Americans suffered on home soil.

As the generations change, we lose something of the personal nature of these events. Aunt Jane has died. But some of the symbols—especially the battle flag of the Confederacy—retain their ability to excite, to challenge, to shame. Descendants of defeat, today's wavers of the battle flag both honor and desecrate the memory of warriors of another time.

Downtown Little Rock is a treat for architecture and history buffs. The Depression-era Robinson Auditorium (BELOW), named for Senator Joe T. Robinson, has hosted everything from Broadway shows to wrestling matches, while the old county courthouse (RIGHT), completed in 1889, was the first courthouse built by Pulaski County. A decade earlier, the Little Rock Catholic diocese started building St. Andrew's Cathedral (OPPOSITE) but didn't finish the structure until a nearby Masonic temple was completed because church powers wanted to make sure the St. Andrew's spire was higher.

BILL PARSONS

MATT BRADLEY

*I*F THE CIVIL WAR CREATED AN ATTITUDE IN THE DEFEATED SOUTH, IT WAS THE POSTWAR PERIOD THAT CULTIVATED AND TENDED THAT ATTITUDE. THE NATURE OF RECONSTRUCTION IN THE SOUTH BY REPUBLICANS IN NATIONAL AND STATE GOVERNMENTS LED TO RESENTMENT AND EVEN BLOODSHED. SOMETIMES the bloodshed even occurred within the Republican ranks, notably here in Little Rock during the Brooks-Baxter War in 1874. The State House served as the primary backdrop to a struggle in which the city became an armed camp, with federal troops trying to preserve order and President Ulysses S. Grant finally recognizing Elisha Baxter, rather than Joseph Brooks, as Arkansas' governor. This would not be the last time a local problem required federal troops and presidential involvement.

A number of African-American legislators came to serve at the State House and, late in the century, watched as we passed the Jim Crow laws, returning the state to a political situation that was as close to the antebellum period as the 13th Amendment to the Constitution would allow. The real and perceived humiliations of defeat hung around the State House like a shroud. It was during this period, the last quarter of the 19th century, that Little Rock transformed itself into a modern city. The city built upon legacies of Reconstruction—which included, with not always fiscally prudent attempts at municipal improvement, the invigorating presence of carpetbaggers and the initiation of real public education for students of both races. Better roads and bridges, lighting, water, and sewers all became a part of a maturing community.

Improvement districts proved to be a valuable tool in facilitating such work as the struggle against the old town branch, which regularly flooded portions of downtown. When citizens of Little Rock's eighth ward, north of the river, felt that they weren't sharing in all of the city's progress, Representative William C. Faucette quietly maneuvered a law through the General Assembly allowing the north shore to proclaim legal independence from Little Rock. We awoke one day in 1904 to find a separate municipality over there. The shock was enormous. Little Rock citizens felt compelled to rush over the river and reclaim the city's fire engines and the like.

In 1911, with the state government needing larger quarters, the General Assembly left the old State House and moved west to a high spot that formerly held the state prison. Some cynics moaned about the decline in the neighborhood. After all, it was here that the legislators affirmed Prohibition, proposed the death penalty as punishment for golfing on Sunday, and passed several racist laws in an unfortunate knee-jerk reaction to the Central High crisis. However, it was also here that representatives affirmed women's suffrage and tackled education reform. The drama afforded by the Assembly regularly unfolds every two years, with special unfoldings at the governor's pleasure. The State Capitol is a grand and handsome building, with the only disappointment being that you can't go up into the dome as you can in the great cathedrals of Italy. It would be quite a view.

BILL PARSONS

The Arkansas State Capitol (OPPOSITE), completed in 1914, was constructed on the site of a former penitentiary—which used to be a funny incongruity but has become less so in recent years. Drawing an equal number of visitors is the marker for the outcropping that explorers named la petite roche, *or the little rock, to distinguish it from a large bluff across the river (ABOVE).*

▼ JAN WILSON JOROLAN

In the spring the woods around Little Rock erupt in a gentle blizzard of dogwoods—not to mention azaleas, crape myrtles, forsythias, and jonquils. These blossoms are a signal for locals to take to the lakes, the rivers, and the hiking trails.

THERE HAVE BEEN, THROUGHOUT OUR HISTORY, SIGNIFICANT MOMENTS WITH BOTH POSITIVE AND NEGATIVE ASPECTS. EVERY WAR HAS STIMULATED SOME KIND OF BOOM. IMPORTANT PEOPLE, PLACES, AND THINGS HAVE APPEARED IN EVERY DECADE. WHAT'S SO SPECIAL ABOUT TODAY? AND, AS MUCH TO THE POINT, HOW in the heck can we know without the passage of time, which gives us that invaluable historical perspective? Well, I'm at least as much a mystic as a historian, and today feels right to me. We seem to have achieved the right balance between the old river town and the big city.

One amazing moment occurred in the history of the newly revived Park Plaza Mall, when a covey of Tibetan Buddhist monks carefully poured colored sand into a complex and beautiful picture. The year was 1991, and these peaceful but alien-looking people were cruising the cultural centers of the United States, looking for sympathetic folk—and, of course, their money—to support them in exile from their native land. In most communities this three-week-long process of pouring sand occurred in a museum or other withdrawn location, but in Little Rock local Buddhists had arranged for the monks to follow their ritual in the city's newest temple of commerce. The event was witnessed by true believers, the curious, and passersby—and somehow it all worked. On their stop before Little Rock—San Francisco—the monks had been encamped at the DeYoung Museum, and some unsettled visitor had messed up the intricate sand mandala upon which the monks had been working. It made the national news. The monks' visit to Park Plaza didn't, but that's just because people don't like good news.

The point is, for a town of fewer than 200,000 Little Rock has some big-city tendencies. We're big enough to host the Rolling Stones and open-minded enough to carry a quietly progressive tradition that has nurtured generations of the city's inhabitants. There exists a

BUDDY MAYS / TRAVEL STOCK

tolerance and a critical mass for a variety of interests and orientations, music, drama, eso-teric thought, and religious practices.

A keeper of the flame was the old *Arkansas Gazette*—the *Gazette* of J.N. Heiskell—which presumed to hold the community to a higher standard than we normally met. It appears that, in many ways, we have internalized the lesson. The torch was passed on to the *Democrat-Gazette* when Heiskell's publication came out on the losing end of a newspaper war. In addition to borrowing from the loser's name, the surviving paper accrued the *Gazette*'s lineage—"since 1819"—in the deal.

In 1996 the Repertory Theater's presentation of *Angels in America*, the Pulitzer Prize-winning extravaganza, gave us a nice look at our accepting selves. The Little Rock production, one of only seven initially authorized for companies throughout the United States, was brilliant, the acting excellent, and, reactions ranged from adulation to "Well, what's the big deal?" No controversy at all.

A corollary to this tradition is the openness of Little Rock "society." Whereas some southern cities require families to be established for generations before they are "one of us," in Little Rock, as one local sage notes, a well-placed $10,000 can get an unconnected newcomer an invitation to any dinner party in town. The money is, of course, for charity, and the ready acceptance stems less from money or lineage, I should think, than from an affection for others who share your cause. This active commitment to civic and arts institutions has created what has been called a service elite in Little Rock. (Unfortunately, the folks with the biggest bucks in the community have yet to establish a solid tradition of proportional generosity to these institutions.)

This white-tailed fawn lives in a hardwood forest near Lake Maumelle just outside town. Cute as he is, the annual pursuit of his parents is one of Arkansas' most honored rituals. In fact, entire businesses close down while men go hunting.

ONE FROM THE HEART

Another big-city tradition is fine dining. But it wasn't always so in Little Rock. For gourmands the turning point came in June of 1975, when Restaurant Jacques et Suzanne opened high in the First National Bank Building. Previously, aside from basic regional fare, we had fed on foreign food from Canton Tea Garden, Polyasian, or Bruno's Little Italy. Well, there had been Breier's and some other pretty good eat shops, but our whole culinary aesthetic expanded with Jack and Suzie's. Finally, we had excellent continental cuisine, which brought the deserved praise of almost all who tasted, including those snooty Manhattanite friends who, before J and S, could only appreciate our barbecue. Jacques et Suzanne's principals themselves left town quickly, unaware of the remarkable seed they had planted. Any number of wonderful restaurants and bakeries sprouted in the culinary soil they fertilized, as employees and inspiration spread from J and S to Andre's, St. Moritz, Prego, Le Casse Croute, 1620, Graffiti's, Alouette's, Ciao's, Kelley's Bistro, Ashley's, and even the Purple Cow. Several chains also realize Little Rock's good taste, and add a variety of national or regional fare to the mix. Round the offering out with a real sushi bar and some terrific Middle Eastern and Oriental establishments, and Little Rock stands proud as a fine place to eat out—and it still has great barbecue!

Of course, eating in can be pretty fine here too. There remains a persistent residue of the old days, when dads made all the money and moms were expected to do everything else. Lots of families carried on a strong tradition of good food, and women who might not have touched a pot or pan before marriage suddenly became real cooks—after several years of experimenting on their unsuspecting families. I'm embarrassed to confess that in my raw and unfeeling youth my brothers and I received some kind of perverse culinary satisfaction when my father's ulcer acted up and Mom had to return to quiet, simple, less imaginative food. That is one of those early food memories imprinted on my brain, with another being the incredible fact that we children were never served anything but leftovers! I know this for a fact. Never. The only compensating factor: Leg of lamb is always better the second time around.

Wild game gives us one of our best opportunities for culinary accomplishment. Even in the city you are known by what you kill, and the most popular prey are ducks and deer. Facets of society seem to shut down during these hunting seasons: There are men who live to hunt, and everything else involves packing up or winding down. Some of the women-folk get down and shoot, some cuss and moan, and some just can't wait for the next season to begin (it gets the men out of the house). Many people of both sexes can entice some of the absolutely finest flavors from their quarry. It's hard to be a vegetarian in this land of delicious wild things.

▲ BUDDY MAYS / TRAVEL STOCK

The trout fishing in northwest Arkansas is considered the nation's finest, but you don't have to go far outside Little Rock to wet a hook and kick back till the perch and crappie start nibbling. And if a hook's not all you want to wet, there's a great old swimming hole just off Highway 10.

ABIG CITY HAS TO HAVE TRANSPORTATION, AND ALTHOUGH WE USED TO SERVE AS A MAJOR PASSENGER RAIL CENTER WITH CONNECTIONS ALL OVER THE COUNTRY AND BEYOND, NOW WHAT WE HAVE IS ANEMIC AMTRAK. ON THE OTHER HAND, FOR A TOWN OF OUR POPULATION, THE 40-PLUS DAILY airline departures from Adams Field are impressive, especially when compared to some of our regional friends. There is also a tradition of adventuresome travel from our town. For example, we were the first city in the United States to send a group to postwar China. The cynic might claim that we must travel to fit something of interest into our bleak lives, but I prefer to think that the richness of life at home requires equally rich experiences away for our travelers.

◀ MATT BRADLEY

While boasting about our big city, I can here acknowledge another characteristic—how 'bout that big-city crime? At least the crime is not as bad as "Gang Banging in Little Rock"—the award-winning HBO documentary—claimed. Indeed, I sat up and took notice when Steve Nawojczyk, a true Little Rock hero, talked about our problems to a national cable TV audience. Driving right by my house, he told viewers how the folks living here didn't go a night without hearing gunshots. The truth is much less dramatic, but the problem is real, especially for young African-American men.

▶ JAN WILSON JOROLAN

Crime is a problem, and a related one is the allocation of resources. Our town may be too big for our own population. Thirty years ago the city held 4,200 people per square mile; today the number is 1,600. We are more spread out and, some would say, spread thin. We expanded using irrefutable logic: We wanted to preempt the "city killers," those smaller municipalities that grow up around cities, stealing tax base and affluent population. But providing services over such a broad area strains resources and whatever unity the city might possess. Real estate influences have pushed attention to the west and have yet to be balanced by other forces. But maybe the Coalition of Little Rock Neighborhoods can provide a little counterweight. The signs are good.

The most remarkable event in this city in recent memory was the vote for the River Project—to build the River Market, expand the convention center, and erect an arena. Proposals to levy a tax for the arena had failed in two previous public referenda, and I bemoaned the missed opportunity; if only people with vision were blessed with money too. But the River Project, which earned support from neighborhoods, and from the eight mayors of Pulaski County, included an arena in, of all places, North Little Rock. When we make up with the old eighth ward, something must be going right. The river separating these twin cities has been a gulf between the "real" city and "dog town" for generations. What miracle allowed us to see that our futures are inextricably tied together, just as downtown is tied to Chenal Valley?

A former Chicagoan who moved to town says he heard about Cajun's Wharf restaurant even in the Windy City. Little Rock has a surprisingly vibrant café life for a city its size, including such favorite seafood hot spots as Cajun's Wharf and Landry's (ABOVE). If you want to know what'll be fresh on Saturday night, you can often spot local chefs picking up produce Saturday morning from the old farmers market downtown (OPPOSITE).

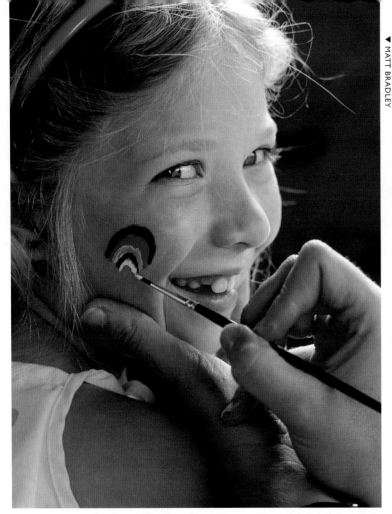

▼ MATT BRADLEY

▼ MATT BRADLEY

In Little Rock there's always something going on that is geared just for kids. At the annual Riverfest (ABOVE), they can get painted up like their former-flower-children parents or clown around to their hearts' delight. At the Art Center's Party in the Park (OPPOSITE RIGHT), kids receive early training in the fine art of graffiti. And during Zoo Days (OPPOSITE LEFT), they can walk and talk with the animals.

It is not coincidental that we have just gone to a ward system for most of our city board. Isn't it a sign of our political maturity that we are recognizing and accepting the presence of constituencies and the need to exercise political power? While guided by the objective management instituted in the 1950s, power politics seemed to be an aberration that occurred only on occasion. Looking back, we see that those occasions happened whenever one of the "powers that be" wanted something that "proper" management wasn't ready to provide. The ward system accepts that power will be exerted and gives it a structure to follow.

AND WITH ALL THESE REALIZATIONS, WE HAVE CLOCKED IN ON OUR DEFINING MOMENT. WE HAVE AS CONTEXT A HISTORY OF MIXED BLESSINGS AND A TRADITION OF MATURING THROUGH THEM. WE HAVE SOME HEALTHY BIG-CITY ATTITUDE IN OUR MEDIUM-SIZED SOUTHERN TOWN. WE HAVE A grand movement tying the region together in the most fragile part of the city—its old heart. We have a political system more ready to respond to everyone. But what flowers blossom in this rich humus we've turned? What is happening in the city that will grow us our defining moments?

The events are coming fast and furious. Five of our major cultural institutions are transforming themselves with capital improvements: the nationally recognized Arkansas Arts Center, growing larger and stronger in its collection of original works of art on paper; the Arkansas Territorial Restoration Museum, with its pioneering living history program and its unique commitment to the collection and study of the work of Arkansas' 19th-century artists and artisans; the Arkansas Museum of Science and History, anchoring the corner of

MATT BRADLEY

JAN WILSON JOROLAN

the east Markham development with exciting exhibits; the old State House, historically the most important structure in the state; and the Wildwood Opera Theater, with the new facility named in honor of Lucy Cabe. New institutions—the Arkansas Children's Museum in the train station and the Aerospace Education Center with its IMAX Theater—give added dimensions to the public programming available to the city.

Other institutions are in the planning stages. The Arkansas Military Museum, slated to occupy the Arsenal in MacArthur Park, will give continued life to an important structure. The Central High Museum will tell the story of 1957, with attention to how the proper telling will help us today. The National Dunbar Alumni Association, a fascinating creation in its own right, is developing a fine traveling exhibit about Dunbar to remind the world that, before Central High, there was excellent education available for African-Americans in Little Rock. A museum featuring African-American Arkansans is also planned, and the Mosaic Templars Building, which once housed the largest African-American fraternal organization in the country and anchored the old Ninth Street commercial district, is set for renovation.

Much has been made of the problems in the city's school district, yet excellent students still flow through the system, gaining a real education in the process. The special example is, of course, Central High itself. A recent survey of top-rated colleges around the country ranked Central as one of the 26 public high schools in the nation that best prepare their students for college. An alliance of concerned citizens, with Chamber of Commerce President Everett Tucker III at the head, has recently committed to the betterment of public education in Little Rock.

Few people took notice in 1995 when a Realtor specializing in downtown houses decided to change professions. But the job switch represented a maturation of the Quapaw Quarter neighborhood. The residential real estate market there has never been better. "They don't need me any more," the Realtor said. Neighborhood groups, the growth of the preservation ethic in Hillcrest, and the renewed support of historic preservation by the city give Little Rock's older sections more hope than they have had in years.

Some of our defining moments seem to stretch out. Does anyone remember a time when a crane didn't loom over the Arkansas Children's Hospital like a big skinny bird accumulating a larger and larger nest? The same goes for the University of Arkansas Medical Sciences campus. With the fine physicians and hospitals in Little Rock, it's a darned good place to get sick. And the old LRU—frequently called Last Resort University—is now the important and growing UALR (that's University of Arkansas at Little Rock), with community involvement making a difference.

This laundry list of good stuff could go on and on. We have a fine symphony; real bookstores; beautiful people; minor-league baseball; impressive corporate offices; friendly dogs; pleasant sailing and nearby fishing; good, but no longer transcendent, Christmas decorations; occasional tornadoes; vital places of worship; fancy dancers; occasional snow in the winter; and always chiggers in the summer.

Our community is full of action—it's called life. Maybe every accurate picture is a little blurred. As to our defining moments, it's our role to experience them. And Little Rock is doing a good job of giving us a place to try. ❧

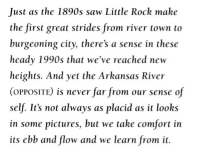

Just as the 1890s saw Little Rock make the first great strides from river town to burgeoning city, there's a sense in these heady 1990s that we've reached new heights. And yet the Arkansas River (OPPOSITE) is never far from our sense of self. It's not always as placid as it looks in some pictures, but we take comfort in its ebb and flow and we learn from it.

PAGES 30 AND 31: WESLEY HITT

MATT BRADLEY

MATT BRADLEY

MATT BRADLEY

BILL PARSONS

DIXIE KNIGHT

In Little Rock, summer becomes official a bit earlier than in other places. Riverfest kicks off just after school's out, giving kids and parents a welcome long weekend of fun down by the riverside. Crafts, crowds, blues, and brews—it's the summertime place to be.

DIXIE KNIGHT

Little Rock's playgrounds are busy year-round, with pickup games and organized leagues. Runners have miles of shady streets to explore, and several times a year they can test themselves in a 5K race, competing against athletes from all over.

Reflections of greatness: Amid the mirrored city, local round ballers take part in the annual Hoop Fest. For one weekend, downtown Little Rock becomes a massive basketball court—and the players become luminous reflections of Scottie, Michael, and Shaq.

The Arkansas State Capitol is said to bear such a close resemblance to the U.S. Capitol that several filmmakers have shot their "Washington" movies in Little Rock. In the early 1990s the gold dome was releafed, at a cost of $61,000. The florid rotunda echoes the intricacies of the Capitol rose garden—or is it vice versa?

▲ WESLEY HITT

▲ MATT BRADLEY

▲ BUDDY MAYS / TRAVEL STOCK

BILL PARSONS

BILL PARSONS

WESLEY HITT

Little Rock has a proud military history—Douglas MacArthur was born here, and troops from nearby Jacksonville Air Force Base saw action, most recently, in the Middle East. Not surprisingly, Veterans Day finds vets from many wars paying tribute to fallen comrades. Mount Holly Cemetery (TOP LEFT AND RIGHT) and the Military Memorial Cemetery (BOTTOM) reflect that honored tradition.

JAN WILSON JOROLAN

MATT BRADLEY

JAN WILSON JOROLAN

For institutions that are supposed to be separate, church and state can sure bear a strong resemblance—and both forces are amply represented in Little Rock. Trinity Episcopal (TOP LEFT) and First United Methodist churches (BOTTOM LEFT) are two of the city's most venerable houses of worship, while the old Pulaski County Courthouse (RIGHT AND OPPOSITE) presents a newly refurbished face on the county's history of government.

MATT BRADLEY

MATT BRADLEY

Little Rock old and new: As far back as the 1870s, the Capital Hotel (OPPOSITE) provided the most luxurious lodgings in town. It declined in this century but was brought back to its former status in the 1980s. Meanwhile, the city has kept the contractors busy—Pavilion in the Park (TOP LEFT), the Excelsior Hotel (TOP RIGHT), and Park Plaza shopping mall (BOTTOM) are three of the town's newest landmarks.

JAN WILSON JOROLAN

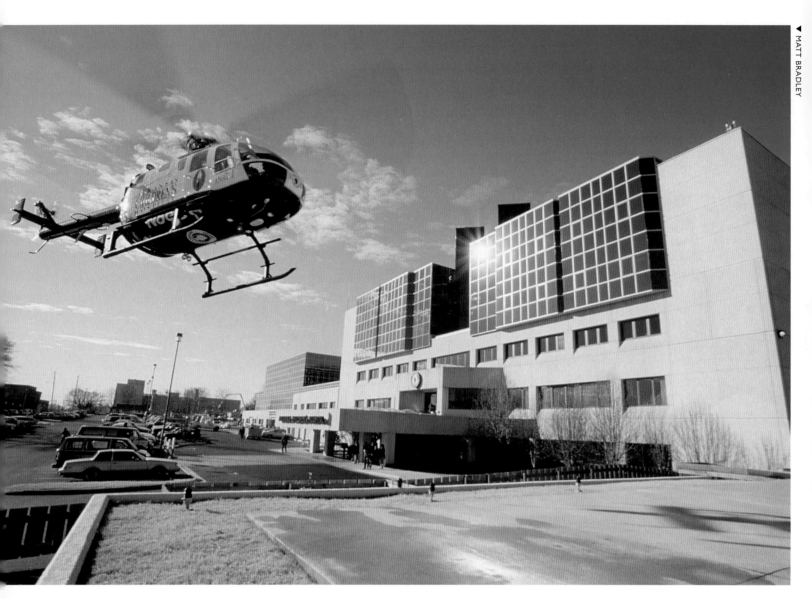

▼ MATT BRADLEY

The bad news is that the skies seem increasingly heavy with helicopters bearing emergency patients. The good news is that the Arkansas Children's Hospital is among the finest medical facilities in the nation to take care of those patients.

DIXIE KNIGHT

DIXIE KNIGHT

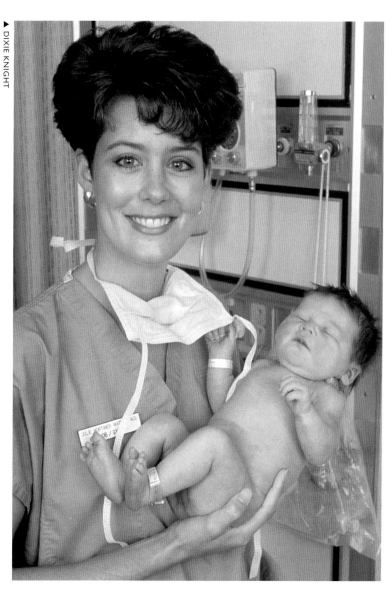

DIXIE KNIGHT

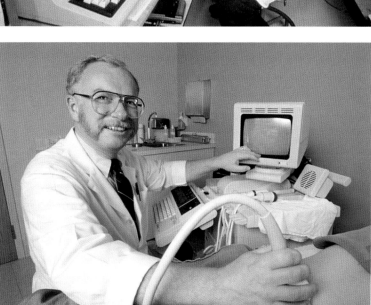

The University of Arkansas for Medical Sciences (UAMS) is another of Little Rock's outstanding medical institutions. World-renowned research and the most advanced systems in such fields as OB-GYN are only two ways in which UAMS delivers.

MATT BRADLEY

The next generation gets its learning both formally and informally. Here, a ranger at Pinnacle Mountain west of the city teaches children about the great outdoors.

DIXIE KNIGHT

MATT BRADLEY

MATT BRADLEY

JAN WILSON JOROLAN

Carver Magnet School (TOP LEFT), *University of Arkansas at Little Rock* (TOP RIGHT), *and Philander Smith College* (BOTTOM RIGHT) *are but a handful of the city's fine educational centers. Some kids also learn to debate with their hands* (BOTTOM LEFT).

WESLEY HITT

Three things children will never stop loving—the messiness of bubbles at a riverside park, the cuddliness of animals at a local livestock fair, and the unbridled go-wildness of games like T-ball.

When the Arkansas Razorbacks play in
Little Rock's War Memorial Stadium,
something happens to otherwise rational
people. How else to explain the wearing
of hog hats and the calling of pigs?

Are there any quainter words than "State Fair"? Every September, it's a week of magic for city kids and farm kids alike—not to mention their parents. In the 1920s the Arkansas fair was held in War Memorial Park, then known as Fair Park. Later it moved to its present home, the fairgrounds on Roosevelt Road (PAGES 54 AND 55).

PAGES 54 AND 55: MATT BRADLEY

*The bookends of a long day in the capital
city: Sunset over the Capitol echoes
sunrise on Markham Street.*

WESLEY HITT

WESLEY HITT

MATT BRADLEY

BILL PARSONS

WILLIE ALLEN

WILLIE ALLEN

*If you judge a city by its devotion to culture, Little Rock passes all tests. The Arkansas Repertory Theater (*TOP RIGHT*) rates among the best in the country, while the Children's Repertory Theater (*TOP LEFT*) keeps the well of talent primed. If it's music you want, just name your tune: the Arkansas Symphony (*BOTTOM LEFT*) or live rock, blues, and jazz at any number of local night spots (*BOTTOM RIGHT*). Ballet Arkansas (*OPPOSITE*) uplifts with amazing grace.*

▼ WESLEY HITT

▲ DIXIE KNIGHT

Make a joyful noise—every Sunday morning (and Sunday night and a whole lot of Wednesdays too) people in Little Rock gather in the city's houses of worship to do just that.

BUDDY MAYS / TRAVEL STOCK

A writer who moved to town from
another state says he loves the quirky
independent spirit of Arkansas. Here, on
the outskirts of Little Rock, a woman
displays her plastic jug fence. And near
North Little Rock a young girl cuddles
up to her dad's antique auto collection.
Still a bit of work to do on those cars.

BUDDY MAYS / TRAVEL STOCK

Situated at the gateway to the West, Little Rock makes a natural railroad center. The Missouri Pacific yard north of the river has been a regional hub serving a dozen states. And wherever there's a river and a railroad, there's a strong industrial district—Little Rock's "backstage."

▶ WESLEY HITT

▲ BILL PARSONS

▲ BILL PARSONS

▲ DIXIE KNIGHT

▲ DIXIE KNIGHT

At the Old Mill in North Little Rock, the visitors and the seasons come and go with the slow steady rhythm of a churning wheel (OPPOSITE). If this picturesque mill looks familiar, it's because you saw it in Gone with the Wind. Rent the movie and visit Arkansas.

Equally as beautiful to visitors is Little Rock's nature show, featuring passionflowers (TOP) and crocuses (BOTTOM).

Long before the first white men visited these parts in 1541, Native Americans inhabited the area. East of Little Rock you can see ancient, gently sloping mounds (ABOVE) attributed to the "Plum Bayou People," who dominated east-central Arkansas from 750 to 950 A.D.

In recent years an amalgam of Native Americans has staged pow-wows in MacArthur Park (OPPOSITE), celebrating the Museum of Science and Industry's exhibit on Native American cultures.

BUDDY MAYS / TRAVEL STOCK

Just off Scenic Highway 7, which runs north-south, you can soak up the natural beauty of the Natural State. Cedar Falls paints a pretty picture in Petit Jean State Park (OPPOSITE). *At Long Pool State Park, canoeists can enjoy the Big Piney River from up close* (ABOVE).

WESLEY HITT

Driving by the river or any Arkansas
lake, even the strongest souls are
tempted to trade in their cellular
phones for a fishing rod.

MATT BRADLEY

Little Rock and its across-the-river neighbor, North Little Rock, have long maintained separate identities, but the new riverfront development may form the sturdiest bridge yet between the two cities.

NAT'L BRADLEY

The McClellan-Kerr River Navigation System opened up the Arkansas River to navigation in the late 1960s. Above, the Little Rock lock and dam. Opposite, a loaded barge and a worker at the locks. Wonder how many times a day he jokes about his dam job?

▲ BRETT LILE

▲ WILLIE ALLEN

▲ WESLEY HITT

▲ DIXIE KNIGHT

▲ WESLEY HITT

When fall brings a nip in the air and a lifesaving reduction in humidity, almost no one can stay inside. Whether you're sailing or fishing or trick-or-treating or kicking leaves in the park, autumn is a great time of year. These ducks look forward to fall too, because when hunting season starts, they'll become the outdoor activity of choice.

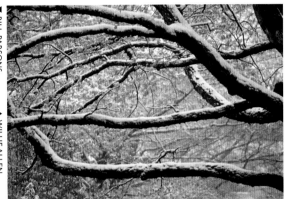

From the sublime to the ridiculous: A gentle snow coats the old State House and outlines slender limbs all over town. Meanwhile, at the Osborne mansion, Mitzi, Breezy, and Jennings still wish for a red Christmas. But since their neighbors sued to ban their light display, this becomes a snapshot of "The Ghosts of Christmas Past."

BILL PARSONS ▶ WILLIE ALLEN ▶ WILLIE ALLEN

BRETT LILE ▶

79

▼ BILL PARSONS

▼ JAN WILSON JOROLAN

DIXIE KNIGHT

MATT BRADLEY

Spring brings garden and house tours, and in the old Quapaw Quarter downtown, the gingerbread is just as tasty as it was 100 years ago. Two featured houses of the Quapaw Quarter are the Turner-Ledbetter home (BOTTOM) and the Rozelle-Murphy home (OPPOSITE, BOTTOM).

JAN WILSON JOROLAN

JAN WILSON JOROLAN

JAN WILSON JOROLAN

BILL PARSONS

Spring also means field trips, and they're not restricted to children. Popular sites in the area include (CLOCKWISE FROM ABOVE) *the courtyard of the Arkansas Arts Center; the grounds of MacArthur Park, named for the general; and the Museum of Science and History, with its fascinating exhibits.*

BILL PARSONS

MATT BRADLEY

WILLIE ALLEN

*Proud of its eventful history, Little Rock
strives to preserve the past. Ten-Mile
House, built 10 miles outside Little Rock
circa 1836, is said to be the first brick
home constructed in the territory* (TOP
LEFT). *The Territorial Restoration is a
living museum where visitors can learn
about the culture of the prestate era,
1820-1836* (BOTTOM LEFT AND RIGHT).

▲ WESLEY HITT

▲ WESLEY HITT

▲ BILL PARSONS

▲ BILL PARSONS

▲ BUDDY MAYS / TRAVEL STOCK

The Little Rock Zoo, located in War Memorial Park, got its start after several animals were left behind following the 1926 State Fair. For a while, the animals were housed in temporary pens until the Works Progress Administration built permanent zoo buildings during the Depression.

Village People: As symbolized by its heartland location, Little Rock thrives on the diversity of America itself. We encourage this diversity and are strengthened by it.

▼ BILL PARSONS

▼ BUDDY MAYS / TRAVEL STOCK

▼ DIXIE KNIGHT

MATT BRADLEY

BUDDY MAYS / TRAVEL STOCK

MATT BRADLEY

ONE FROM THE HEART

▼ BUDDY MAYS / TRAVEL STOCK

▲ BILL PARSONS

▲ BUDDY MAYS / TRAVEL STOCK

*No matter what you're fishing for—bass
or business—it doesn't hurt to drop a
line in the Arkansas River at Little Rock.
Who knows? You might even win the
tournament.*

PROFILES

A LOOK AT THE CORPORATIONS, BUSINESSES, PROFESSIONAL
GROUPS, AND COMMUNITY SERVICE ORGANIZATIONS THAT HAVE
MADE THIS BOOK POSSIBLE. THEIR STORIES—OFFERING AN
INFORMAL CHRONICLE OF THE LOCAL BUSINESS COMMUNITY—ARE
ARRANGED ACCORDING TO THE DATE THEY WERE ESTABLISHED IN
LITTLE ROCK.

IN EXCELLENCE

PAGES 90 AND 91: BILL PARSONS

PAGE 92: WESLEY HITT

SOUTHWESTERN BELL TELEPHONE COMPANY

WITH DEREGULATION THE CURRENT WATCHWORD IN THE COMMUNICATIONS INDUSTRY, SOUTHWESTERN BELL TELEPHONE COMPANY FACES AN ERA OF COMPETITION FOR RESIDENTIAL AND BUSINESS TELEPHONE SERVICES. BUT EVEN IN THESE CHANGING TIMES, THE COMPANY'S STRATEGY FOR MAINTAINING ITS POSITION AS THE CLEAR INDUSTRY leader in Arkansas is the same one it employed more than a century ago—supplying high-quality, affordable, dependable service that includes the latest in technological advancements.

THE EARLY DAYS

Attracting business customers was a major goal of Jasper N. Keller when he came to Little Rock in early 1881. Along with Little Rock banker Colonel Logan H. Roots, Keller formed the Southwestern Telegraph and Telephone Company. With the exclusive rights to the use of Alexander Graham Bell's telephone patent in both Arkansas and Texas, Keller and Roots set about developing a unified telephone system for the two states.

By 1883 the company had 36 exchanges in the territory and 4,214 telephones. Keller and Roots then sold the company to an eastern organization known as the Lowell Syndicate. In 1917 the Arkansas exchanges were sold by Southwestern Telegraph and Telephone to Southwestern Bell Telephone Company of Missouri.

Today Southwestern Bell provides voice, data, and video services to more than 850,000 access lines in Arkansas. The company's 2,800 Arkansas employees provide superior personal service with advanced technology and a competitive attitude.

In recent years the company has placed a strong emphasis on rolling out new voice, data, and video services, such as the popular Caller ID service. Southwestern Bell also is a leader in developing distance learning, which allows resource sharing between schools in Arkansas, and Telemedicine, the use of interactive video and high-speed data transmission to allow remote diagnosis, radiology services, and medical training.

COMMITMENT TO THE FUTURE

Southwestern Bell's leadership role today is demonstrated by its commitment to technology. The company launched a $231 million investment plan that began in 1993 as Arkansas set its sights on becoming one of only three states in the nation to be fully digital, making it possible for business and residential customers to transmit high-quality voice, data, and video at any distance in a matter of seconds.

Fiber-optic technology is another critical component of Southwestern Bell's ability to provide Arkansas customers with quality service. The company has been installing fiber-optic lines throughout the state since the early 1980s and has more fiber-optic miles than any other telecommunications provider in Arkansas. Fiber optics help provide customers with a fail-safe self-healing system that automatically reroutes calls when there are equipment problems to ensure no call gets lost. The addition of fiber-optic lines not only benefits Arkansas residential customers, but has also been a factor in the relocation of several businesses to Little Rock.

The specter of competition for basic local telephone service presents strategic challenges for Southwestern Bell Telephone Company, but none more daunting than those Keller and Roots faced as they worked to bring Arkansas its first unified telephone system. In this century or last, the strategy remains the same: the best in telecommunications at a reasonable price.

▶ MARK BALDWIN

Distance-learning technology is a two-way interactive video link provided over telephone lines. The technology enables a teacher from one location to teach classes at another site or allows students from several schools to access the same instructional programming.

St. Vincent Infirmary Medical Center

*f*ROM THAT FIRST DAY IN 1888 WHEN FIVE SISTERS OF CHARITY FROM NAZARETH, KENTUCKY, OPENED ST. VINCENT HOSPITAL, THE FACILITY HAS KEPT ITS EYE ON THE FUTURE WHILE WORKING HARD TO IMPROVE HEALTH CARE FOR ALL ARKANSANS. INNOVATIONS IN PRODUCTS AND SERVICES HAVE REMAINED THE PRIMARY EMPHASIS AT WHAT IS KNOWN TODAY AS ST. VINCENT INFIRMARY

Medical Center for more than 100 years, as the facility has grown from 10 beds housed in a converted residence to a 717-bed acute care hospital.

St. Vincent continually measures and assesses the needs of the community and provides a holistic approach to health care—the hospital's 2,700 employees are truly committed to maintaining the tra-

needs staffed by two primary care physicians and three nurses. St. Vincent-North also offers full-service medical imaging, laboratory testing, cardiology lab facilities, office space, and a conference center. Phase 2 calls for a surgery center and additional diagnostic services. St. Vincent is helping develop medical facilities in west Little Rock, downtown Little Rock, and Cabot.

Project Guardian Angel has become a model for statewide efforts to raise immunization levels. In May 1995 the program received national recognition during the 29th National Immunization Conference in Los Angeles.

Mobile Heart Clinic
Another off-site contribution St. Vincent makes to the overall health

ABOVE: St. Vincent-North was opened in 1995 to extend top-quality, affordable health care into north Pulaski County, the towns of Cabot and Lonoke, and other areas along the Highway 67-167 corridor.

ABOVE RIGHT: In 1995 St. Vincent became a regional positron-emission tomography (PET) imaging center, allowing doctors to see accurately inside the human body in a noninvasive way.

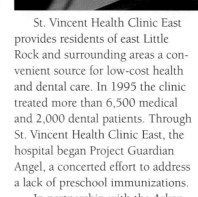

dition of caring as a way of life. As proof of that commitment to excellence, St. Vincent has introduced a host of new products and services over the past few years.

Expanded Service Area
In 1995 St. Vincent-North was opened to extend top-quality, affordable health care into north Pulaski County, the towns of Cabot and Lonoke, and other areas along the Highway 67-167 corridor. A 65,000-square-foot medical office building and outpatient center, St. Vincent North is located in Sherwood and is being developed in phases. Phase 1 includes occupational medicine, which is being provided through HealthFirst, a clinic for minor health care

St. Vincent Health Clinic East provides residents of east Little Rock and surrounding areas a convenient source for low-cost health and dental care. In 1995 the clinic treated more than 6,500 medical and 2,000 dental patients. Through St. Vincent Health Clinic East, the hospital began Project Guardian Angel, a concerted effort to address a lack of preschool immunizations.

In partnership with the Arkansas Health Department and the Department of Human Services Child Care Licensing Section, the project provides on-site immunizations against childhood diseases for children at selected day care centers. More than 1,000 children were immunized at 29 centers in the program's first two years, and

of the community is through its mobile cardiology outreach efforts, whereby Arkansas Heart Institute (AHI) diagnostic technicians travel as many as 200 miles a day to provide echo, stress, holter, EKG, and other noninvasive cardiology testing in outlying areas. The mobile, high-tech cardiology clinic allows patients to avoid a trip to Little Rock and enables AHI to perform diagnostic studies at physicians' satellite clinics. Continued development of fiber-optic telephone services may eventually enable the AHI technicians to transmit test results directly to St. Vincent for additional analysis and consultation.

In 1995 St. Vincent became a regional positron-emission tomography (PET) imaging center, serving physicians and other hospitals in a 350-mile radius of Little Rock with the latest innovation in diagnostic equipment. PET allows a doctor to see accurately inside the human body in a noninvasive way. Unlike X-ray, ultrasound, or MRI—which show only the structure of bones, organs, or tissues—PET enables doctors to monitor the level of an organ's function to detect the presence of disease. The technology allows a physician to examine the heart, brain, liver, tumors, and muscle tissue by charting the distribution of positron-emitting radioactive material through the body.

WOMEN'S CANCER RECOVERY CENTER

Taking treatment several steps further and giving it real-life application is the goal of St. Vincent's new Women's Cancer Recovery Center. The center consolidates all the services a woman needs to help her through the trials of breast cancer. The Women's Cancer Recovery Center offers prosthesis fitting and wardrobe consultation; prosthesis and mastectomy bras; free wig and hairstyling; makeup consultation; a print and video library to lend educational materials; computer-based instruction; a support group for patients and their families; individual consultations for dietary, fitness, and psychosocial needs; and a variety of social events. These services are provided at no charge to women as long as resources permit.

Another extension of St. Vincent's commitment to excellence is Healthstar Ultima-The Arkansas Health System. Healthstar is a fully integrated health care network designed to place high-quality, cost-effective health services within easy access of all Arkansans. The Healthstar network is projected to include more than 1,000 physicians and 20 to 25 hospitals within six months.

OCCUPATIONAL MEDICINE PROGRAM

MedWorks is St. Vincent's occupational medicine managed care organization, which offers businesses and industries a system of loss control by helping move an injured employee through the health care system from the moment of injury to his or her return to work. MedWorks services include health screenings, work site evaluation, safety and wellness instruction, injury treatment, and workers'

compensation consultation. The program serves as a liaison with the employee, the physician, the hospital, and the employer to manage escalating workers' compensation costs and provide a quicker return to work.

All these innovations speak clearly to the mission of St. Vincent Infirmary Medical Center and its commitment to reaching out to the community it serves with a variety of accessible, affordable health care services.

CLOCKWISE FROM ABOVE: *From that first day in 1888 when five Sisters of Charity from Nazareth, Kentucky, opened St. Vincent, the hospital has kept its eye on the future while working hard to improve health care for all Arkansans.*

Arkansas Heart Institute (AHI) diagnostic technicians travel as many as 200 miles a day in their mobile facility to provide echo, stress, holter, EKG, and other noninvasive cardiology testing in outlying areas.

Emergency facilities at St. Vincent Infirmary Medical Center provide the critical care patients need.

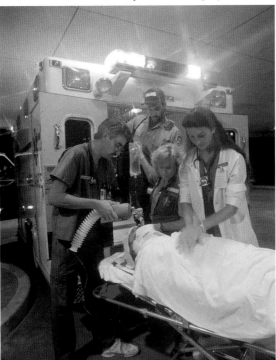

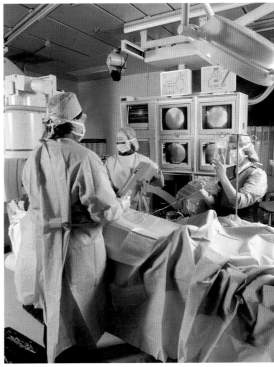

Harry L. Ehrenberg & Associates, Inc.

To say that Harry Ehrenberg Jr. has followed in his ancestors' footsteps would be accurate, but a little misleading. Each Ehrenberg generation—of which Harry Jr. is the fourth—has redefined the agency that began in 1899 as one of the city's first casualty insurance operations. His father, Harry Ehrenberg Sr., sold the casualty side

of the business to concentrate on estate and retirement planning. He also led the agency into the securities business. Ehrenberg Jr. has built on his family's insurance and finance backgrounds to shape Harry L. Ehrenberg & Associates, Inc. into a firm that specializes in negotiating settlements of personal injury lawsuits and investing the proceeds of those settlements, as well as assisting businesses and families in addressing insurance and investment issues.

Expert on Settlement Options

"Insurance sales traditionally have been a what-if situation," Ehrenberg says. "What does it mean financially if you die? What does it mean financially if you are disabled? In the cases I am involved in, the what-if has already occurred. I know how to get a

family back on its feet financially after a tragedy."

For that reason, attorneys often bring in Ehrenberg to help evaluate settlement alternatives consisting of either payments over time from the defendant or a single payment to the plaintiff to be invested. Both alternatives have their advantages as well as their drawbacks and must be evaluated in light of the family's overall situation. Of particular concern for many is the ability to remain eligible for government benefits such as Medicaid.

Working with Families

The 17 years Ehrenberg has spent specializing in working with people who have already faced the what-if have helped him develop a sensitivity that he applies to his work with those who have yet to suffer such tragedy. "A significant amount of my time is still spent working

with families establishing life insurance and investment programs. When they are trying to make decisions like 'How do I protect my family if I die?' 'How do I maintain my standard of living if I'm hurt?' or 'What is the best way to invest for my retirement?' I've already been through those situations with people who have had to face them," he says. "That insight is what I can bring to the table."

In all his work with families, Ehrenberg stresses the fundamentals of sound personal finances. To that end he has developed The Financial Navigator, a process that helps a family assess how well their financial affairs are in order. "Our nation's economic system—the free enterprise system—rewards efficient management. What I strive for is finding the most efficient way for a family to manage its finances."

Harry Ehrenberg Jr. has built on his family's insurance and finance backgrounds to shape Harry L. Ehrenberg & Associates, Inc. into a firm that specializes in negotiating settlements of personal injury lawsuits and investing the proceeds of those settlements, as well as assisting businesses and families in addressing insurance and investment issues.

TREADWAY ELECTRIC CO., INC.

ON THE WALL OF TED TREADWAY'S OFFICE HANGS A FRAMED DOCUMENT—THE HAND-WRITTEN LIST OF 14 RULES OF BUSINESS AS LAID OUT BY W.A. AND THEO TREADWAY, TED'S GREAT-UNCLE AND GRANDFATHER. THE COMMONSENSE PRINCIPLES THAT HELPED THEM BUILD THE BUSINESS FOUNDED BY THEIR FATHER, LEO TREADWAY, IN 1905,

still guide the fourth- and fifth-generation Treadways who oversee the widespread operation today.

Through its four locations in Arkadelphia, Pine Bluff, Hot Springs, and Little Rock, Treadway Electric Co., Inc. is committed to providing quality electrical products from quality manufacturers at reasonable prices, more than 400 lines in all. The company provides electrical supplies for commercial, industrial, and residential accounts, as well as for utilities, telecommunications businesses, and poultry processing industries.

CONTINUOUS TRAINING

Treadway Electric's offices are staffed by long-term employees who attend monthly in-house, new-product training sessions with representatives of the leading vendors. The company's sales force is encouraged to attend regional training schools, and all employees are offered the opportunity to attend Dale Carnegie training to make them more effective in communicating with customers.

Many of the products sold at Treadway Electric can also be found at discount merchandisers and home-oriented warehouse operations. But while the large retailers might have those products, they don't have the expertise to sell or explain them, nor the time to commit to the customer. And in the case of an emergency, a member of the Treadway Electric Co. sales staff is available after hours to give quality service 24 hours a day. Another service plus is Treadway's large delivery fleet, which provides free and prompt delivery to customers. The company's daily shuttles between its four Arkansas branches ensure a complete, high-quality inventory at all locations.

FROM THE BEGINNING

After founding Treadway Electric Co., Leo Treadway was subsequently joined by sons W.A. and Theo, both of whom earned master's degrees in electrical engineering from the University of Arkansas, the alma mater for all the Treadways since. Today, along with daughter Amy Treadway, Ted Treadway, the company's CEO and president, guides the family business.

Treadway Electric Company was the state's first electrical distributor, and holds the honor of distributing Square D Company's products longer than any firm in the country. Treadway also was the first distributor west of the Mississippi River to handle the General Electric Lamp line.

Such distinctions have firmly established Treadway Electric Co.'s longtime leadership role in the distribution of high-quality electrical products. The ongoing education and expertise of its sales staff ensure superior service for its customers for decades to come. Innovative business practices are layered atop a rich history—Treadway Electric Co. continues to dedicate itself to its suppliers and its customers the same way its forefathers detailed all those years ago.

The commonsense principles that helped build the business founded by Leo Treadway in 1905 still guide the fourth- and fifth-generation Treadways who oversee the widespread operation today.

ENTERGY CORPORATION

ENTERGY CORPORATION'S NETWORK OF POWER-SUPPLYING COMPANIES IS FAR-REACHING, STRETCHING THE LENGTH OF ARKANSAS, THROUGH THE WESTERN HALF OF MISSISSIPPI, ACROSS SOUTHERN LOUISIANA, AND DEEP INTO THE HEART OF TEXAS. MORE THAN 2.3 MILLION RETAIL CUSTOMERS ARE SERVED BY ENTERGY, MAKING IT THE LEADING ELECTRICITY SUPPLIER

in the Middle South region and one of the largest investor-owned public utility holding companies in the United States.

A HISTORY OF GROWTH

Founder Harvey C. Couch didn't fathom such growth when he formed Arkansas Power Company late in 1913. But just a year later Couch used a sawdust-powered steam boiler to generate enough excess steam to spin two 550-kilowatt turbines on a 22,000-volt, 22-mile power line to connect Malvern and Arkadelphia. The merger of the two cities' electric companies began a pattern of buy-ing properties and building central power stations that would guide Couch's company for years to come.

By 1924 Couch had reached beyond his home state to form Mississippi Power & Light Company and Louisiana Power Company. By 1931 Couch's Arkansas Light & Power Company, as it was now called, was serving 228 cities and towns in Arkansas and, along with Couch's utilities in Mississippi and Louisiana, comprised the operating subsidiaries of Electric Power and Light Corporation, which had been formed as a holding company five years earlier. In 1949 Electric Power and Light Corporation was renamed Middle South Utilities, and in 1989 it became Entergy Corporation—a name derived from the words enterprise, energy, and synergy.

FINDING A HOME IN ARKANSAS

Arkansas plays as important a role in Entergy's present and future as it did in its past. Little Rock is home to Entergy's retail services organization. Six regional customer service centers serving Arkansas, Louisiana, Mississippi, and Texas are always on call, accommodating virtually every customer transaction by phone. From the comfort of home, customers now can do business

BELOW: From its telephone customer service center in Little Rock, Entergy handles customer calls seven days a week.

LEFT: *Entergy's retail services organization develops and markets products, services, and technologies that help customers make their lives more comfortable and convenient.*

ideas for their customers systemwide. Entergy experts use their knowledge to help customers select the energy options most suitable for their needs. Heating and cooling systems for residential and commercial applications, security lighting, water heaters, and new construction technologies provide customers systemwide with a menu of options to improve their comfort, convenience, and security.

Entergy also is investigating the feasibility of such programs as an automatic outage reporting service that would speed repairs and an appliance repair warranty program through which customers could safeguard their appliances. In combination with such exciting marketing pilot programs, these options offer customers a breadth and scope of products and services unparalleled in the energy industry.

Through leadership, innovation, vision in customer service, and marketing, Entergy Corporation creates value for its customers. From Little Rock, Entergy brings value-added solutions based on years of experience and customer-focused flexibility.

with the company when and where it is convenient for them. Automated systems in each phone center enable 24-hour reporting of power outages and fast, efficient dispatching of repair crews. These service centers are linked to Entergy's customer information system and field offices through a high-speed fiber-optic network.

Entergy vehicles equipped with mobile data terminals stay in constant communication with dispatch computers, enabling service requests to flow smoothly along the company's information superhighway. Customers, vendors, and employees send and retrieve information over 2,000 miles of fiber-optic cable, which serves to speed communications and increase reliability. Electronic mapping of all the equipment in the system provides the information necessary to monitor and improve maintenance.

SERVICE TOPS THE LIST

Knowledge is power, and when it comes to energy lifestyle products and services, Entergy is a powerful company. Using years of experience, expertise, and flexibility, Entergy marketing professionals in Little Rock provide innovative

LEFT: *Entergy's service trucks now travel the information superhighway using mobile computer terminals that help speed service response to customer requests.*

FEDERAL RESERVE BANK OF ST. LOUIS—LITTLE ROCK BRANCH

WHEN THE FEDERAL RESERVE SYSTEM WAS CREATED BY CONGRESS IN 1913, THE IMMEDIATE CHALLENGE WAS TO ENSURE A SAFE, EFFICIENT MONETARY PAYMENT SYSTEM THAT WOULD BRING ABOUT SUSTAINABLE ECONOMIC GROWTH AND STABLE PRICES. TODAY THE CHALLENGES FOR THE FEDERAL RESERVE ARE NO LESS DAUNTING.

Federal Reserve Banks operate a nationwide payments system to provide certain financial services to financial institutions, the United States government, and foreign official institutions. The banks also conduct monetary policy in pursuit of maximum employment, stable prices, and moderate long-term interest rates. Finally, the Reserve Banks supervise and regulate banking institutions to ensure the safety and soundness of the nation's banking and financial system and to protect the credit rights of consumers. The Little Rock Branch functions primarily as a payments system service provider to Arkansas financial institutions.

INVOLVED IN THE NATION'S PAYMENTS SYSTEM

As it has since its founding, the Federal Reserve remains responsible for ensuring the integrity and efficiency of the U.S. dollar payments system. Transactions in the payments system take place using a variety of methods including cash, check, automated clearinghouse (ACH), credit card, funds transfer, and securities transfer—to name only a few.

Cash is the most preferred method for completing transactions in the United States. Reserve Banks put currency and coin into circulation for the Treasury, and as cash flows back to the Federal Reserve, each deposit is counted and verified for accuracy and authenticity, and unfit currency and coin are destroyed.

Checks are the next preferred method for completing transactions, with more than 60 billion checks written in the United States each year. The Federal Reserve op-

erates a nationwide check-clearing system that includes processing and transporting checks in paper and/or electronic form from the bank of first deposit to the bank that will deduct the funds from the writer's account.

ACH is an electronic payment delivery system most often used to process repetitive small dollar retail payments. The Federal Reserve first introduced ACH in the early 1970s as a more efficient alternative to checks, and it has grown into a nationwide payment method for electronically originating credit and debit transfers (e.g. payroll, insurance, mortgages, etc.).

New payment options such as debit cards and electronic cash are in the news daily. These services offer convenience and can speed up the completion of a transaction. The Federal Reserve is committed

The Little Rock Branch of the Federal Reserve Bank moved to its current building in May 1967.

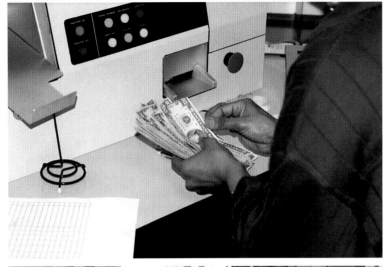

to supporting innovations that remove paper from the payments process, while at the same time maintaining a safe, efficient, and accessible payment system.

REGIONAL RESPONSIBILITIES

Conducting monetary policy begins at the regional level. Each of the 12 Federal Reserve Banks and 25 Branches has its own board of directors. These directors are community leaders who provide monthly reports on their respective industries to the district presidents. The district presidents then discuss this and other economic data at the Federal Open Market Committee meetings where actions on monetary policy are taken. These actions affect the growth rate of the money supply, short-term interest rates, and other economic variables.

Regulation and supervision of banks is one way of reducing the incidence of bank failures and resulting financial panics. The Federal Reserve has primary supervisory responsibility for all bank holding companies, their nonbank subsidiaries, and their foreign subsidiaries; for state-chartered banks that are members of the Federal Reserve System and their foreign branches and subsidiaries; and for the Edge Act and agreement corporations through which United States banking organizations conduct business abroad. A few examples of regulations that the Federal Reserve examiners enforce are the Community Reinvestment Act, Equal Credit Opportunity, Expedited Funds Availability Act, Home Mortgage Disclosure Act, and Truth in Lending Act.

The Little Rock Branch is located in the Eighth District, with the head office in St. Louis. The branch was established on September 14, 1918, and opened for business on January 6, 1919. The Eighth District serves Arkansas, eastern Missouri, southern Indiana, southern Illinois, western Kentucky, western Tennessee, and northern Mississippi.

The Federal Reserve provides financial services only to financial institutions. However, the general public can purchase new issues of government securities through the Little Rock Branch and tours of the branch's operations are available. A tour can be arranged by calling the Personnel Department. Additionally, the Little Rock Branch has an active Speakers Bureau. Federal Reserve staff members speak at schools, clubs, seminars, and civic organizations free of charge.

CLOCKWISE FROM TOP LEFT: *Currency received at the Federal Reserve Bank is counted and verified for accuracy and authenticity on high-speed machines. Bills rejected by this machine are handled individually.*

Millions of checks are received daily at the Federal Reserve. Each check is read by high-speed equipment and sorted by destination for delivery.

Personal computers play a key role in providing the technology necessary to complete electronic payments and financial activities.

Each Federal Reserve Bank has a highly trained protection staff to provide around-the-clock security.

BAPTIST HEALTH

BAPTIST HEALTH WAS FOUNDED IN 1920 AS AN 80-BED HOSPITAL WHOSE LEADERS HAD A DREAM—TO HEAL THE SICK AND ENHANCE THE LIVES OF THE PEOPLE OF ARKANSAS. TODAY, BAPTIST HEALTH IS THE STATE'S LARGEST PROVIDER OF HEALTH CARE SERVICES, DELIVERING QUALITY CARE THAT SPANS A LIFETIME—FROM PRENATAL THROUGH THE GOLDEN YEARS.

The growing Baptist Health network encompasses multiple facilities that address a broad spectrum of health care issues, including education, prevention, organ transplantation, rehabilitation, retirement living for senior adults, and more. All combine to implement a vision of total health for all Arkansans through a continuum of comprehensive programs and services.

Baptist Health was founded in a small building in Little Rock when Baptist State Hospital opened in November 1920 at a temporary site. Construction of the first permanent building began in 1921. The 300-bed facility opened January 1, 1925, offering accessible health care, dedicated to enriching and prolonging human life by de-livering patient-centered care with Christian compassion and personal concern. Since its founding, Baptist Health has remained focused on the philosophy that health care is more than a business—it is a ministry of health and healing.

A LEADER ARRIVES

John A. Gilbreath, a Texan, was hired as Baptist State Hospital's assistant administrator in September 1945 and became hospital administrator a year later. For 38 years, Gilbreath guided the development of a health care delivery network that today leads Arkansas in health care services.

By early 1956, the hospital's name had been changed to Arkansas Baptist Hospital and a $1.5 million construction project had added 137 new beds. In 1959, the hospital was chosen to work with the city of North Little Rock to plan, build, and operate a facility there, and in January 1962, the 118-bed Memorial Hospital opened. The hospital is known today as Baptist Memorial Medical Center to reflect its association with Baptist Health.

Arkansas Baptist Hospital was renamed Arkansas Baptist Medical Center in 1965 as the hospital began negotiations to secure property to move westward. The next year, the board of trustees voted to proceed with the construction of a $20 million medical complex in what was then the western section of the city—the corner of University Avenue and Evergreen Street. A couple of years later, realizing that

Baptist Health has locations across the city, from its hospitals in Little Rock and North Little Rock to its specialty clinics.

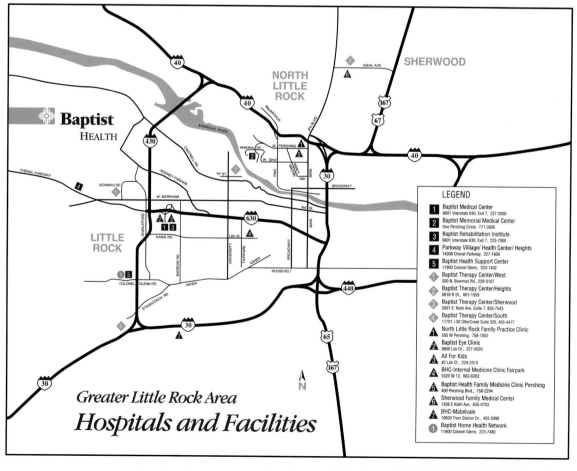

Greater Little Rock Area
Hospitals and Facilities

LEGEND

1 Baptist Medical Center
9601 Interstate 630, Exit 7, 227-2000
2 Baptist Memorial Medical Center
One Pershing Circle, 771-3000
3 Baptist Rehabilitation Institute
9601 Interstate 630, Exit 7, 223-7000
4 Parkway Villiage/ Health Center/ Heights
14300 Chenal Parkway, 227-1600
5 Baptist Health Support Center
11900 Colonel Glenn, 223-7402
1 Baptist Therapy Center/West
200 N. Bowman Rd., 228-0107
2 Baptist Therapy Center/Heights
5618 R St., 661-1555
3 Baptist Therapy Center/Sherwood
2001 E. Kiehl Ave. Suite 7, 835-7543
4 Baptist Therapy Center/South
11701 I-30 OtterCreek Suite 320, 455-4477
A North Little Rock Family Practice Clinic
505 W Pershing, 758-1002
A Baptist Eye Clinic
9800 Lile Dr., 227-2020
A All For Kids
#2 Lile Ct., 224-2313
A BHC-Internal Medicine Clinic Fairpark
5320 W 12, 663-6262
A Baptist Health Family Medicine Clinic Pershing
400 Pershing Blvd., 758-2294
A Sherwood Family Medical Center
1308 E Kiehl Ave. 835-0703
A BHC-Mabelvale
10600 Train Station Dr., 455-5998
1 Baptist Home Health Network
11900 Colonel Glenn, 223-7480

FAR LEFT: *Baptist Memorial Medical Center in North Little Rock is recognized as being among the finest hospitals of its size in the country.*

LEFT: *The Baptist Health main campus covers 213 acres in west Little Rock at the intersections of Interstates 430 and 630. Baptist Medical Center (foreground) and Baptist Rehabilitation Institute (background center) are located on the campus.*

BELOW: *Parkway Village, Parkway Heights, and Parkway Health Center are located on Chenal Parkway.*

the property was landlocked and offered little room for future growth, the board negotiated the purchase of a 213-acre tract that is now known as the Little Rock campus. Ground was broken on the new 534-bed hospital in June 1971 and the new hospital opened in March 1974. The board of trustees voted to call the new facility Baptist Medical Center and change the name of the downtown facility to Central Baptist Hospital.

REACHING OUT TO ARKANSAS

On March 3, 1974, Baptist Medical Center admitted its first patient, the final step in grand-opening ceremonies that included a dedication speech by then-Vice President Gerald Ford. Concurrently, Arkansas Rehabilitation Institute opened as a service of Central Baptist Hospital in response to the national trend toward physical and rehabilitation medicine. When Central Baptist Hospital closed later that decade, Arkansas Rehabilitation Institute became a stand-alone facility.

The 1980s saw a continued outreach, as Baptist Medical Center opened its Outpatient Services Center, and Memorial Hospital began converting space for use by outpatients. In 1981, Baptist Health expanded into southwest Arkansas, entering into a long-

term lease agreement to operate Twin Rivers Medical Center in Arkadelphia.

In 1982, the board of trustees, seeing a need to provide continuing care for senior adults, incorporated Parkway Village. Plans were announced to build cottages and apartments immediately, with intermediate and long-term facilities to be added later.

In 1983, Central Baptist Hospital closed and all acute care services were moved to Baptist Medical Center. A new 57-bed facility at Twin Rivers Medical Center was opened in Arkadelphia. Also, early in 1983, Gilbreath announced that he would retire as chief executive officer at the end of the year, and Russell D. Harrington Jr., who had joined the organization in 1973, became president under a new corporate structure.

In 1984, Baptist Medical Center inaugurated the state's first air ambulance service. Today Baptist MedFlight is Arkansas' best-known service and offers both helicopter and fixed-wing transport. The Baptist MedFlight helicopter is the state's only air ambulance service that makes trauma scene flights.

In the mid-1980s, as the organization began to look for ways to extend its impact beyond traditional acute care, it implemented the VHA Resource Sharing Affiliates

program, which now provides nine Arkansas hospitals access to Baptist Health's management and purchasing resources; opened a home health agency and home medical equipment company; and developed Health Advantage, the state's first hospital-owned and -operated health maintenance organization (HMO).

GROUNDBREAKING HEALTH CARE

In February 1989, Baptist Medical Center performed its first kidney transplant. In November, the first heart transplant in Arkansas history was performed there. And the next spring, the state's first laparoscopic gallbladder removal was performed at Baptist Memorial Medical Center.

ABOVE: *Baptist MedFlight initiated air ambulance service in Arkansas in 1984. Today, it is the state's most widely recognized trauma air ambulance service.*

RIGHT: *The MRI has become a widely recognized technology for diagnosis of disease. Baptist Health operates three MRI units at its hospitals.*

In the 1990s, Baptist Health formed Practice Plus, a physician development and practice management company that currently is developing a primary care network throughout central Arkansas. The organization also joined with Arkansas Blue Cross Blue Shield to form the state's largest HMO when Health Advantage merged with HMO Arkansas. It became the statewide tertiary referral center for Arkansas FirstSource, the state's largest preferred provide organization (PPO), operated by Blue Cross Blue Shield.

The name Baptist Health was adopted in 1995 to better reflect who and what the organization is today, and to mark its long-lasting commitment to its philosophy and vision.

BAPTIST HEALTH

Baptist Health currently operates four hospitals: Baptist Medical Center, Baptist Memorial Medical Center, Baptist Medical Center Arkadelphia, and Baptist Rehabilitation Institute. The organization also operates Parkway Village, Parkway Heights, Parkway Health Center, Baptist Schools of Nursing and Allied Health, Baptist Health Plaza Hotel, eight Baptist Therapy Centers, and more than 20 primary care clinics.

Baptist Medical Center, a licensed 787-bed tertiary care facility, is the largest private not-for-profit hospital in the state. The center is known for its diagnosis and treatment of cardiovascular disease, orthopedic services, organ transplantation program, women's services, ophthalmology services, and helicopter and fixed-wing emergency transport services.

Baptist Memorial Medical Center, a community-owned not-for-profit acute care hospital in North Little Rock, is licensed for 260 beds, including a 16-bed recuperative care unit. Recognized as one of the finest hospitals of its size in the country, the medical center offers services usually found only in larger metropolitan facilities. Plans call for the center to be relocated in 1999 to a site just northeast of the intersection of Interstate 40 and U.S. Highway 67-167.

Baptist Medical Center Arkadelphia is a 57-bed acute care hospital that provides medical care for much of southwest Arkansas. The facility features modern equipment and expanding medical offerings, including outpatient, diagnostic, emergency care, orthopedic, and ophthalmology services.

Baptist Rehabilitation Institute—the state's largest rehabilitation hospital—offers programs such as physical and occupational therapy, speech language pathology, and adolescent psychiatry. The institute also has programs for alcohol and drug abuse, amputation, arthritis, orthopedic spinal cord injuries, and stroke patients.

Parkway Village, an independent living retirement community composed of cottages and apartments on an 87-acre campus, is filled with nature trails, open spaces, and three private lakes. Included at Parkway Village are an elegant dining room and auditorium, a gym, and an indoor swimming pool. The complex features 24-hour medical assistance, security, and emergency call buttons in all bedrooms and baths.

Parkway Heights, a residential care facility added in 1994, completed the continuum of care on the Parkway Village campus. Parkway Heights offers an alternative for people who need more assistance than independent living, but who need fewer services than a long-term care setting. The facility

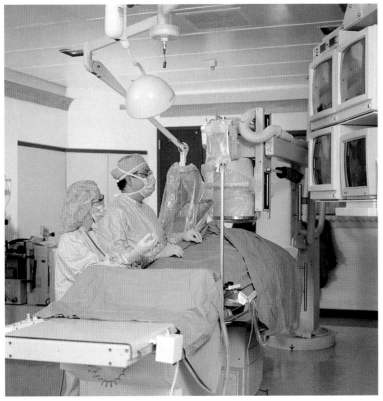

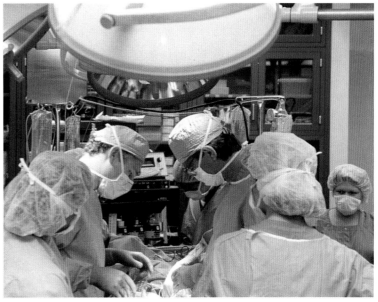

provides a support staff, three meals a day, housekeeping services, and transportation, as well as a variety of apartment options for residents.

Baptist Schools of Nursing and Allied Health provide eight schools for students interested in a health care career, including two nursing school programs.

Baptist Health Plaza Hotel offers families and friends of Baptist patients a comfortable, affordable place to stay. Located on the Baptist Health campus in Little Rock, the hotel offers a wooded jogging trail and free shuttle service to and from the campus hospitals. Guest rooms offer cable TV, filtered air and water, refrigerator, and microwave.

Baptist Therapy Centers bring a full range of outpatient rehabilitation services to patients at eight locations in Arkansas. All offer physical and occupational therapy and speech language pathology.

BAPTIST HEALTH FOUNDATION

The Baptist Health Foundation is the fund-raising arm of the organization, composed of friends and community volunteers who are committed to Baptist Health's values of service, honesty, respect, stewardship, and performance. The foundation is governed by a 27-member board of trustees, all of whom work on a voluntary basis and offer expertise in management and financial affairs. In addition, the foundation depends on volunteers, other foundations, friends, corporations, and businesses for financial resources, skills, time, and spirit that money cannot buy.

The Baptist Health Foundation Board of Trustees, forever mindful of its vital role in obtaining additional financial support for the organization's healing ministry, oversees a variety of fund-raising events and campaigns each year, including the annual Bolo Bash, which includes a dinner and auction, a golf tournament, and a fashion show.

The Circles of Excellence are made up of people who share their time, money, and commitment to support health care delivered with an attitude of Christian compassion and personal concern. The Benefactors Circle serves as the base of support for the foundation, with members annually contributing between $1,000 and $5,000. Members of the Honorary Board of Trustees make a cash gift of $500,000 or establish an irrevocable trust of $1 million.

The foundation began a program of grant awards in 1985 as an expression of support to Baptist Health and its continuing goal of excellence in health care. Through effective fund-raising and financial management, the amount available for awards has increased each year.

FOCUSING ON ITS MISSION

Through the evolution of its facilities and services, and all that goes into maintaining and improving them, Baptist Health has always kept its focus on its primary mission: providing quality patient-centered services, promoting and protecting the voluntary health care system, providing quality health education, and responding to the changing health needs of the citizens of Arkansas with an attitude of Christian compassion and personal concern.

With a new name and a continued commitment to quality health care through the 21st century and beyond, Baptist Health is working to bring total health to all Arkansans.

ABOVE: *Arkansas' first heart transplant was performed at Baptist Medical Center on November 10, 1989. The recipient was Mary Wilson of Jacksonville.*

FAR LEFT: *Cardiologists at Baptist Health hospitals have performed 50,000-plus cardiac catheterizations— more than any other health care provider.*

University of Arkansas at Little Rock

PRACTICALLY HIDDEN AMONG THE TALL PINES THAT BORDER ONE OF THE CITY'S MAJOR THOROUGHFARES IS A UNIVERSITY THAT IS ANYTHING BUT HIDDEN IN THE LIFE OF THE COMMUNITY. THE UNIVERSITY OF ARKANSAS AT LITTLE ROCK (UALR), A YOUNG, THRIVING, METROPOLITAN UNIVERSITY, BELIES THE IVORY-TOWER IMAGE OFTEN ASSOCIATED WITH

institutions of higher learning.

Its academic structure, student body, research activities, and public service programs reflect the issues, challenges, diversities, and realities of contemporary America. Its mission is to achieve excellence within the classroom while also forming community partnerships to solve problems that impact us all.

With this commitment to extend excellence beyond campus boundaries, UALR has grown in its 70-year existence to become a major component of the University of Arkansas system and an integral thread in the fabric of Little Rock's life—impacting its residents not only academically, but culturally as well.

Academics for All Ages

With more than half of all professional people in the state living within a 50-mile radius of Little Rock, UALR recognizes its educational importance to the area. Its 400 full-time faculty offer more than 100 programs leading to associate, bachelor's, master's, and doctoral degrees. But this academic assortment is only part of the picture.

To accommodate a myriad of schedules in today's fast-paced world, the university makes day, evening, and off-campus classes available throughout the year. And, to make lifelong education a reality for all ages, UALR offers special elementary programs such as Summer Laureate/University for Youth; special secondary programs that allow students to explore career opportunities in business and international studies; noncredit courses for adults wishing to learn about everything from backcountry travel to wine tasting; and free tuition for all senior citizens.

A Mosaic of Excellence

At UALR, diversity is the norm within the student body. In a typical daytime class, you'll find recent high school graduates from all over the country sitting alongside 70-year-old retirees, while evening classes add to the campus a large group of professionals seeking career changes or enrichment. And adult students, obtaining degrees after years of other challenges, are always present, along with international students and students with disabilities.

Although it does offer housing for some of its students, UALR is primarily a commuter campus, with 85 percent of its students living nearby and working at least 20 hours a week in addition to taking classes. This mosaic of ages, genders, accents, races, and careers makes UALR a wonderfully tex-

RIGHT: With 85 percent of its graduates remaining in Arkansas and more than half of its students already working part-time while attending class, UALR is a vital link in the state's economic structure.

BELOW RIGHT: Learning enjoyment starts at an early age at UALR thanks to its innovative community partnerships and educational programs.

tured place offering relationships and experiences that are rare at more traditional universities.

REDEFINING SCHOLARSHIP

Because the university is such an active and integral part of the community, its definition of scholarship among faculty has broadened to include not only the scholarship of research and discovery, but the scholarship of integration, application, and teaching, as well. Faculty members are challenged to involve their students in service learning projects that place them in the context of the community, rather than simply creating an insulated academic environment.

One way this is accomplished is through the Friday Fellows program, which awards scholarships and service learning opportunities to 10 junior students each year who demonstrate superior scholarship, leadership, and volunteerism in the community. Faculty also are encouraged to directly apply their research to real problems and challenges that contemporary society faces today, either locally, regionally, nationally, or, in some cases, internationally. As Chancellor Charles Hathaway puts it, "Much of what we will accomplish will depend on our students' extending the creativity and expertise of our faculty to partnerships with our community."

A UNIVERSITY THAT WORKS WITH PEOPLE

Partnerships are the key to UALR's strength and presence in the community, and have been since 1927. As the university has grown, its connection to the community has gone far beyond this initial relationship, and its many public service programs have prompted the creation of the Office of Campus and Community Partnerships.

Some of these programs include a Neighborhood Homework Center with computer stations for children and their parents; a Lit-

Students have the best of both worlds at UALR: a state capital location—filled with opportunities—that still retains the beauty of the natural state.

eracy Corps program in public schools; free testing in the Speech and Hearing Clinic; athletic outreach programs using mentors to address drug abuse and gang activity; and a Partners in the Arts cultural program for the aesthetic enjoyment and enrichment of the entire central Arkansas community.

The campus even houses the Baum Decision Support Center, an electronic meeting room created to assist businesses, governmental agencies, and nonprofit organizations in developing their own strategic plans. In these and other projects, UALR students, faculty, and staff volunteer their time and services, turning great ideas into brilliant and beneficial collaborative realities.

CHARTING THE COURSE FOR THE FUTURE

Tying together the strands of diversity found in UALR's programs of study, student body, and community partnerships is a single mission: To develop the intellect of students; to discover and disseminate knowledge; to serve and strengthen society by enhancing awareness in scientific, technical, and cultural arenas; and to extend the university into the Little Rock metropolitan area to create a model of excellence.

UALR is committed to this quest for excellence—in teaching, in scholarly activities, and in professional service—that will address universal issues, as well as local and regional challenges.

MERRILL LYNCH

*F*OR SOME 70 YEARS, MERRILL LYNCH HAS ADVISED THE PEOPLE, CORPORATIONS, AND INSTITUTIONS OF ARKANSAS AS TO HOW TO BEST ACHIEVE THEIR FINANCIAL GOALS. THE COMPANY BACKED ITS ADVICE WITH A MARKET PERSPECTIVE AND THE PERSONAL SERVICE ITS CLIENTS NEEDED TO SUCCEED. THIS LONG HISTORY OF SERVING ARKANSANS MAKES MERRILL LYNCH THE OLDEST FIRM OF ITS KIND

in the state.

From Merrill Lynch's offices in the TCBY Tower in downtown Little Rock, 80 employees offer customers a wide range of financial services, while another dozen serve institutional clients from the firm's west Little Rock branch. Half of Merrill Lynch's staff consists of licensed financial professionals, while the other half is composed of valuable support members who assist in innumerable ways.

More than 40,000 Merrill Lynch employees serve in 510 offices in 31 countries around the world. The firm also serves 6,000 corporations, institutions, and governments. Its worldwide network of financial consultants, private bankers, and product specialists serves more than 4 million individual clients and more than 400,000 small to midsize businesses and institutions. These numbers add up to one impressive

reality: Merrill Lynch serves more individuals, companies, and countries with more financial advice, underwritings, and transaction executions in more markets across more borders than any other firm in history.

PUTTING THE CUSTOMER FIRST

The son of a small-town Florida doctor, Charles E. Merrill, founder of what is today known as Merrill Lynch, studied at Amherst and the University of Michigan before moving to New York to work in the business office of a textile firm. While he was there, he struck up a friendship with Edmund Lynch, who was selling soda fountain equipment. Early on, Merrill had some different ideas about the investment business. Believing that the opportunities of the market should be accessible to everyone, he set about his life's work—bringing Wall Street to Main Street.

Merrill established the firm in 1914, and 16 months later added Lynch to the company and the letterhead.

In addition to promoting the accessibility of the market, Merrill espoused a philosophy of putting clients' interests first. And since the days decades ago when Merrill Lynch first brought Arkansas its wide array of services, the firm has continued to be built on that strong yet simple tenet.

Today that customer-first philosophy is expressed in five principles that define the way Merrill Lynch does business: client focus, respect for the individual, teamwork, responsible citizenship, and integrity. Those principles are the standards by which Merrill Lynch measures the thousands of decisions the firm's employees make every day and the means by which the firm achieves success for its clients, its shareholders, and, in turn, itself.

Merrill Lynch's financial consultants stress planning with a well-conceived written document that considers a broad range of financial needs. The firm's consultants help clients define their financial goals, determine the amount of time they have to reach those goals, and establish their performance expectations. The consultants also work to tailor comprehensive strategies for managing clients' total portfolios—assets and liabilities—to help accommodate major transitions in their business and personal lives.

SERVING THE WORLD

Merrill Lynch clients are served primarily through two business units: the Private Client Group and the Corporate and Institutional Client Group. The Private Client Group provides planning-based financial management services, including in-

vestment services, private banking, retirement and group employee benefit services, insurance, home financing, personal credit and business-financing services, trust services, estate planning, and financial portfolio planning. This group serves more than 4 million households, small to midsize businesses, and regional financial institutions through a branch office network of more than 13,000 financial consultants. Worldwide, retail clients had entrusted $703 billion of their assets to Merrill Lynch at the end of 1995.

The Corporate and Institutional Client Group consists of several divisions designed to supply personal financial services to larger corporations and other entities through investment banking, institutional client services, institutional investment management services, and global client products, which build on Merrill Lynch's leadership in product development and market-making activities.

Another unit of Merrill Lynch—Merrill Lynch Asset Management (MLAM)—serves clients worldwide as one of the largest mutual fund companies in the world. MLAM had more than $164 billion in client assets under fee-based management at the end of 1994. The group offers more than 200 fixed-income, equity, and money market mutual funds as well as providing asset management services to a wide range of institutions and individuals.

The firm's Global Securities

Research and Economics Group includes a staff of almost 150 fundamental equity analysts—based both in the United States and globally— that covers more than 60 major industry categories worldwide. The Merrill Lynch Fixed Income Research team is composed of about 75 analysts who provide institutional and retail sales forces with current information on investments and securities markets.

Merrill Lynch has had a global presence for more than 45 years. By the end of 1994 more than 11 percent of the firm's employees were located outside the United States. Merrill Lynch maintains full

membership on the principal exchanges in the United States, London, Tokyo, Toronto, Frankfurt, Hong Kong, Sydney, Luxembourg, Singapore, Zurich, and Mexico.

The breadth of services Merrill Lynch offers and the worldwide scope of its operation are due to the same principles that Merrill laid out decades ago and the same credos that have driven the firm's Little Rock office since the 1920s— to understand clients' financial needs, educate them about their choices, and help them make informed financial decisions.

From Merrill Lynch's offices in the TCBY Tower in downtown Little Rock, 80 employees offer customers a wide range of financial services, while another dozen serve institutional clients from the firm's west Little Rock branch.

AMERICAN AIRLINES

THE LITTLE ROCK AIRPORT WAS NOTHING MORE THAN A TINY LANDING STRIP WHEN AMERICAN AIRLINES FIRST TOUCHED DOWN THERE ON JUNE 15, 1931. THE FIRST AIRLINE TO SERVE LITTLE ROCK WITH PASSENGER AND AIRMAIL SERVICE, AMERICAN AIRLINES REMAINS A LEADER IN THE MARKET TODAY, GIVING PASSENGERS THE SAME PROMPT, SAFE, AFFORDABLE SERVICE THEY'VE

come to expect over the many decades American has operated here.

American Airlines along with its regional partner, American Eagle, offers nonstop service from Little Rock to Dallas/Fort Worth. The daily service to Dallas/Fort Worth allows Little Rock passengers a quick, affordable, and convenient way to connect with flights to business and leisure destinations around the world.

Some 48 employees work in American Airlines' offices in Little Rock, doing everything from dispensing tickets to handling baggage to cleaning and servicing airplanes. Others work in the convenient

Agents with American Airlines in Little Rock display their community support in T-shirts that say, "I'm Big on Little Rock." Some 48 employees work in American Airlines' offices in Little Rock doing everything from dispensing tickets to handling baggage to cleaning and servicing airplanes.

American Airlines ticket office in Pavilion in the Park, the centrally located shopping complex on Cantrell Road where customers can purchase tickets, make reservations, and handle air-travel business. Many of the American Airlines employees in Little Rock have been with the company as many as 30 or 40 years, ensuring an unbroken string of quality customer service.

THE EARLY DAYS

American Airlines had been in operation only two years when it first began to serve Little Rock. From dozens of companies, a holding company called the Aviation Corporation was formed in 1929. All of the subsidiaries were incorporated in 1930 into American Airways. Routes were redrawn and management reorganized. A cancel-

lation by the government of airmail contracts brought the fledgling company to a halt in 1934, but a couple of months later, when new contracts were let, American Airways became American Airlines Inc., and the new company emerged with a more integrated route system. The airline pioneered the development of an air traffic control system later adopted by all airlines and administered by the U.S. government.

Although dependent on airmail during the early 1930s, American Airlines realized that the future of air travel lay in the development of passenger service. The breakthrough came with the introduction of the famed Douglas DC-3, which American inaugurated with a Chicago-to-New York flight in June 1936.

The company has continued to upgrade its fleet over the years, in

1949 becoming the only airline in the United States with a completely postwar fleet of pressurized passenger airplanes, in 1953 pioneering nonstop transcontinental service, and adding the latest in Boeing jet aircraft beginning with the 707 in 1959.

CONTINUING INNOVATIONS

The innovations have continued through the years. American has remained a major player in the cargo business, offering same-day service. The company developed the Semi-Automated Business Research Environment (SABRE), a computerized reservations system used today by more than 29,000 travel agencies in 74 countries. American Eagle was formed in 1984 to satisfy the need for smaller, commuter flights; it now offers more than 1,300 flights a day to nearly 150 cities.

Today American Airlines and American Eagle provide service to more than 260 cities through a combination of jet and turboprop service, offering its passengers the same convenience, safety, and affordability that have been a hallmark of the airline—in Little Rock and beyond—for decades.

Arkla

THE 20TH CENTURY WAS A MERE INFANT OF FIVE WHEN ARKLA FIRST BEGAN DISTRIBUTING NATURAL GAS TO CUSTOMERS. WITH THE 21ST CENTURY AROUND THE CORNER, ARKLA HAS BECOME AN INTEGRAL PART OF NORAM ENERGY CORP., A NATIONAL LEADER IN ENERGY DISTRIBUTION, SERVICE, AND MARKETING. IN FACT, ARKLA WAS THE WELLSPRING FOR THE FORMATION OF NORAM—THE

third-largest natural gas distribution company in the country and one of the largest pipeline companies in the world. NorAm provides the public a complete menu of energy services, including gathering, supply, storage, transportation, and wholesale electric services.

Arkla and NorAm offer complete energy management services and can help businesses develop specific plans to effectively and efficiently meet customer needs. Arkla customers in Arkansas, Louisiana, Oklahoma, and Texas can rest assured that Arkla will provide dependable natural gas service at the most reasonable rates possible, with safety always uppermost in the minds and actions of Arkla associates.

ENERGY RESOURCES FOR THE 21ST CENTURY

Through its affiliation with NorAm, Arkla has the resources that will help provide industrial and commercial customers the finest energy services as they move into the new century. For example, natural gas fueled vehicles are now in operation in Little Rock. U.S. Postal Service vehicles and city and state government fleets are being converted to natural gas, as are the vehicles in Arkla's motor pool. Vehicles powered by natural gas will help take the pressure off oil exploration as the nation's fossil fuels grow

scarcer, while reducing emission problems that threaten the ozone and the atmosphere in our cities and other urban areas.

Arkla was instrumental in implementing the Clean Cities program in Little Rock. Now one of 40 such cities nationwide, Little Rock is committed to the expansion of fuels that promote clean air.

But despite its innovative technology and state-of-the-art energy equipment, Arkla is well aware that its success is based on customer loyalty. Arkla strives to earn the support of its business and residential customers through value-added customized solutions to energy needs, and by listening to its customers.

Part of this effort to serve Arkla's customers in a pleasing and satisfactory way is geared toward adequate training for its more than 1,500 associates, including 330 in the Little Rock area. And, while technical skills are vital to its associates, Arkla also encourages them to practice excellent customer relations skills. Arkla recognizes that part of this desired attitude by its associates is based on their belief that Arkla is a good place to work.

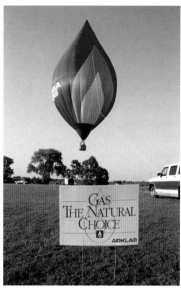

A COMMUNITY PRESENCE

Community service has been at the top of Arkla's priority list since beginning to serve customers 90 years ago. Arkla's associates are encouraged to take leading roles in their communities through United Way campaigns, Red Cross blood drives, American Cancer Society, Arthritis Foundation, American Heart Association, and Easter Seals.

Arkla helps meet the energy needs of low-income families. Arkla's Good Neighbor Fuel Fund has helped pay for natural gas service for some 12,000 low-income senior citizens, the disabled, families on fixed incomes, and others with financial problems since it began in 1988. Funded by employee and customer contributions, the fund is matched by Arkla up to $5,000 each month.

From its headquarters in downtown Little Rock, through communications and by example, Arkla's top management conveys to its associates in four states that Arkla's obligation is to its customers, its communities, and its associates. Arkla is dedicated to sharing the warmth neighbor to neighbor.

CLOCKWISE FROM FAR LEFT: *President and COO Mike Means guides Arkla today.*

Arkla is an integral part of NorAm Energy Corp., a national leader in energy distribution, service, and marketing.

Arkla has the resources to provide industrial and commercial customers the finest energy services as they move into the new century.

Arkla is well aware that its success is based on customer loyalty.

ALLTEL Corporation

More than 50 years ago, two former Southwestern Bell employees, Hugh Wilbourn Jr. and Charles Miller, decided to strike out on their own and purchase the former Grant County Telephone Company. That company, whose assets consisted primarily of 275 telephones and a toll line running from Pine Bluff to Sheridan, Arkansas, became the forerunner of what would eventually become ALLTEL Corporation—one of the nation's key providers of telecommunications and information services.

ALLTEL Corporation now serves nearly 2 million local telephone lines in the South and Midwest; more than half a million cellular customers, primarily in the Sunbelt; and more than 1,100 information services clients around the globe. The company, whose 1995 revenues exceeded $3 billion, employs 16,000 people—including more than 3,000 in Little Rock.

Headquartered in Little Rock

ALLTEL, headquartered in Little Rock, was officially formed in 1983 by the merger of two regional telephone companies known as Mid-Continent Telephone Corporation of Hudson, Ohio, and Allied Telephone Company of Little Rock—whose early roots included the former Grant County Telephone Company, founded in 1946.

Building on its solid base of telephone operations, the company has selectively expanded into related markets over the past decade, including cellular telephone service and information services. The result is balanced diversification in a number of good markets.

Providing Telephone Service

ALLTEL's telephone operations serve nearly 2 million customer lines across the South and Midwest, making ALLTEL the nation's 11th-largest telephone company

Clockwise from top left: ALLTEL's telephone operations serve nearly 2 million customer lines across the South and Midwest.

ALLTEL's cellular service areas include Little Rock and other growing metropolitan areas such as Charlotte, North Carolina, and Gainesville, Florida.

Around the world, ALLTEL's information services products help financial institutions make the strategic decisions required in today's complex global markets.

Through its retail outlets, including three in the Little Rock area, ALLTEL Mobile offers the latest in cellular phones and accessories.

PHOTOGRAPHY BY ERIC MYER PHOTOGRAPHY, INC.

and fourth-largest non-Bell telephone company. ALLTEL serves more than 93,000 customers in Arkansas—including Glenwood, Harrison, Crossett, and Greenbrier. One hundred percent of the company's telephone customers in Arkansas are served by state-of-the-art digital technology. ALLTEL, which is known as a quality, efficient operator of its markets, has invested more than a billion dollars in its network over the past decade.

ENTERING THE CELLULAR MARKET

ALLTEL entered the cellular market in 1983. Since that time ALLTEL Mobile's customer base has grown to include more than half a million customers. The company's cellular operations are concentrated in predominantly fast-growing southern markets including Little Rock, Fort Smith, and Fayetteville, Arkansas; Charlotte, North Carolina; Gainesville/Ocala, Florida; and Augusta, Savannah, and Albany, Georgia. ALLTEL's cellular markets include approximately 8.2 million "pops," an industry gauge of potential customers.

INFORMATION SERVICES

ALLTEL Information Services was founded in Little Rock in 1968 by three data processing managers

who—frustrated about having to develop their own software systems—formed a software development cooperative. Since that time the company has grown from a supplier of information processing services and software for the banking market into a major provider of information-based solutions to the financial, telecommunications, mortgage, and health care industries. The company serves more than 1,100 clients around the globe including NationsBank, Chase, Citibank, GTE Mobilnet, BellSouth Cellular, New York University Medical Center, National Institutes of Health, and Baystate Health System.

DIVERSIFIED VENTURES

In addition to its three primary business units, ALLTEL has several other operations and investments.

Distribution businesses owned by ALLTEL include ALLTEL Supply, a provider of telecommunications and data products, headquartered in Atlanta; and HWC Distribution Corp., a supplier of specialty wire and cable, headquartered in Houston. ALLTEL also owns approximately 7 percent of WorldCom, Inc. (formerly LDDS Communications, Inc.), the nation's fourth-largest long-distance service provider; and operates ALLTEL

Publishing Corporation, which produces telephone directories for the company's telephone subsidiaries and other telephone companies nationwide. ALLTEL's other operations include wide-area paging services.

RECOGNIZED GROWTH

Over the past several years, ALLTEL has enhanced earnings growth by selectively expanding from its core telephone business into faster-growing markets. The cellular and information services businesses now generate a significant portion of the company's earnings.

This performance has been recognized and the company is now ranked not only on the Fortune 500 and Forbes 500, but also on the Standard & Poor's 500 index.

Such growth has benefited the company and the city of Little Rock. Over the past five years, ALLTEL has created more than 1,400 new jobs in the community and significantly expanded its offices. The company now occupies more than one million square feet of office space in Little Rock.

The company and its employees are also recognized as good corporate citizens, participating in many local volunteer efforts.

ABOVE LEFT: *The Technology Center in west Little Rock serves ALLTEL's information services clients and is one of the most advanced information processing centers in the nation.*

ABOVE RIGHT: *Even though many of ALLTEL's telephone customers live in rural and suburban areas, they can depend on the same high-quality, reliable phone service available in larger cities.*

PHOTOGRAPHY BY ERIC MYER PHOTOGRAPHY, INC.

JACUZZI BROS.

JACUZZI® BROS. PRIDES ITSELF ON MANUFACTURING MANY OF THE MOST INNOVATIVE PRODUCTS OFFERED IN THE POOL/SPA INDUSTRY, AS WELL AS THE WATER SYSTEMS INDUSTRY. WITH MORE THAN 60 ORIGINAL PATENTS AND A RECORD OF CONTINUOUS IMPROVEMENTS, JACUZZI BROS. TAKES CREDIT FOR MANY INDUSTRY FIRSTS—FROM THE INVENTION OF THE REVOLUTIONARY JET PUMP TO THE MORE RECENT CREATION of the Ring-lok access design that made servicing Jacuzzi pool/spa pumps and filters faster and easier than those of the competition.

AVIATION BEGINNINGS

The company actually got its start in the aviation business when the seven Jacuzzi brothers came to America from Italy and began manufacturing propellers in the San Francisco Bay area in 1915. The company flourished throughout World War I as a supplier for the U.S. Air Force, but when the end of the war brought a sharp reduction in the demand for props, the company turned to aircraft design.

In 1921, only one year later, Jacuzzi received national acclaim by building the first fully enclosed, multipassenger cabin monoplane ever flown in America. That same year, however, the Jacuzzi family ended its aviation association after one of the brothers was killed during a test flight—but this was not the end of the brothers' commitment to innovation.

In 1925, while conducting experiments in fluid dynamics, Rachele Jacuzzi hit on the idea of moving water with water, the principle that led him to invent the jet pump. Rachele Jacuzzi's discovery not only altered the course of the company, setting it on the path to worldwide success, but it also revolutionized the pump business.

Soon after, Jacuzzi Bros. began expanding its product lines to make a wide variety of water systems pumps. In 1955 the company also expanded into the swimming pool market, offering a complete line of equipment to the growing swimming pool industry. Throughout the years, the company has continued its tradition of innovation with products like the marine jet propulsion unit, which was used by the U.S. Navy during the Vietnam War.

In addition to Jacuzzi Bros.' renowned line of products, its sister company Jacuzzi Whirlpool Bath is credited with the invention of the first fully self-contained whirlpool bath, which created that industry.

INNOVATIVE PRODUCTS ARE JACUZZI'S HALLMARK

Today Jacuzzi Bros.' line of pool and spa equipment includes a variety of pumps, filters, filter accessories, skimmers, and jets. Innovation continues to be at the core of these products with features such as Jacuzzi's unique Ring-lok access design, which allows quick-and-easy no-tool servicing and maintenance.

The most recent advancements in the pool side of the business include the new Landslide D.E. filter with a patented wiper plate design, which allows for more efficient D.E.

BELOW: The seven Jacuzzi brothers left their home in Casarsa, Italy, to seek their fortune in America.

BELOW RIGHT: Since 1915 Jacuzzi Bros. has been defining quality products.

regeneration and longer filter cycles, and the new Tri-C.L.O.P.S. Element filter with its three uniquely shaped patented elements that ensure the pool owner can "Clean Less Often Per Season" and save time, chemicals, water, and electricity.

Water systems equipment produced in Little Rock today includes submersible pumps, jet pumps, utility pumps, centrifugal pumps, sump and sewage pumps, noncorrosive pumps, tanks, and accessories.

A revolutionary product in the water systems division, the Jacuzzi Sandhandler submersible pump was the first of its kind to utilize plastic parts when they were introduced in the 1950s. Superior performance is provided by Jacuzzi's patented eye and hub seal, which offers exceptional resistance to sand-related wear and failure.

Jacuzzi Operations

Jacuzzi Bros. moved its international headquarters to Little Rock in 1963 to accommodate a more centralized distribution. The company is situated on 43 acres and operates a 250,000-square-foot manufacturing and distribution complex. In addition to sales in all 50 states, Jacuzzi Bros. also has sales in 50 foreign countries.

Jacuzzi Inc., based in Walnut Creek, California, is the parent company of Jacuzzi Bros., as well as Jacuzzi Whirlpool Bath in Walnut Creek; Jacuzzi Canada in Ontario; Jacuzzi do Brasil in Ito, Brazil; Jacuzzi Chili in Santiago, Chile; and Jacuzzi Europe S.p.A. in Pordenone, Italy. Jacuzzi Inc. is a subsidiary of U.S. Industries, Inc., a diversified industrial manage-

ment corporation located in Iselin, New Jersey.

Jacuzzi Supplies the World

State-of-the-art products are not the only way Jacuzzi sets itself apart. A progressive, innovative team of more than 250 employees are committed to the company tag line, "Making a Difference." Each department strives to stay abreast of the latest and most effective ways of doing business so that

Jacuzzi can best serve its customers.

Innovation has been the watchword of Jacuzzi Bros. since the aviation-oriented days decades ago in California. It remains at the forefront in all aspects of the Little Rock operation as Jacuzzi Bros. supplies the world with the newest and the best in water systems and pool and spa equipment.

ABOVE: *Jet pumps are still built at Jacuzzi Bros.' 43-acre manufacturing and distribution facility in Little Rock.*

ABOVE LEFT: *Innovation has always been the watchword of Jacuzzi Bros.*

LEFT: *The Tri-C.L.O.P.S. filter is just one of Jacuzzi's latest innovations in the pool/spa division.*

SMITH FIBERGLASS PRODUCTS INC.

Smith Fiberglass Products Inc. has been headquartered in Little Rock for more than three decades, but its position as one of North America's leading manufacturers of reinforced fiberglass pipe and fittings gives it a worldwide sphere of influence. From its beginnings as a pilot plant in Milwaukee in the mid-1950s, through its incorporation in 1961 and its move to Little Rock in 1963, Smith Fiberglass has banked its future on fiberglass pipe and the unique noncorrosive properties it offers. Three decades of experience have shown that fiberglass pipe is an excellent choice to carry everything from crude oil, salt water, acids, and chlorides to natural gases, carbon dioxide, salts, and solvents.

Such versatility has made fiberglass pipe the leader for customers as varied as oil and gas producers, the pulp and paper industry, the chemical process industry, gasoline service stations, industrial plants, the mining industry, chlorine-caustic plants, power plants, fertilizing manufacturing plants, steel mills, the food processing industry, air-conditioning companies, water and wastewater facilities, and oil refineries.

ABOVE: *From its beginnings as a pilot plant in Milwaukee in the mid-1950s, through its incorporation in 1961 and its move to Little Rock in 1963, Smith Fiberglass has banked its future on fiberglass pipe and the unique noncorrosive properties it offers.*

RIGHT: *Industries' needs for larger-diameter fiberglass pipe systems prompted Smith Fiberglass to open a second, 45,000-square-foot facility in Little Rock devoted to the production of 18- through 48-inch pipe and piping systems.*

ATTRACTED TO LITTLE ROCK

As the market grew for fiberglass pipe, the need for a high-volume production facility attracted Smith Fiberglass to Little Rock, with its abundant and eager labor force. The original plant has seen several expansions, and today employees at the 243,000-square-foot facility manufacture composite products, specializing in low-pressure piping systems from one to 16 inches in diameter.

Industries' needs for larger-diameter fiberglass pipe systems prompted Smith Fiberglass to open a second, 45,000-square-foot facility in Little Rock devoted to the production of 18- through 48-inch pipe and piping systems. More than 350 employees work in the two Little Rock locations, and 150 more are employed in the Wichita plant, which became part of the Smith Fiberglass team in 1987 with the purchase of a Kansas pipe com-

pany. In 1996 the company opened its first overseas plant, a joint venture, in Harbin, China, to service the oil fields of northern China.

Staying close to the customer is a critical element in the pipe business. More than 20 Smith Fiberglass employees are in the field, consulting with engineers, selling the company's products through distributors, and training those

who install the piping systems. At one point, Smith Fiberglass had technical personnel on simultaneous installations in the Baltics, Brunei, Kuwait, and South America.

RECOGNIZED FOR QUALITY

Throughout its history, Smith Fiberglass has pursued third-party quality certification for its products. In 1968 the company received the first Underwriters Laboratories Listing for nonmetallic piping conveying petroleum fuels underground. Its piping systems have met industry specifications,

procedures, and standards set by the American Society for Testing and Materials, the American Petroleum Institute, the American Water Works Association, NSF International, and others.

Smith Fiberglass Products was the first fiberglass pipe manufacturer in North America to be registered to the International Organization for Standardization's ISO

9001 standard for quality. It was also the first fiberglass pipe manufacturer to be certified to the American Petroleum Institute's Specification Q1.

From its longtime home base of Little Rock to its most remote installation operation in the backcountry of Argentina, Smith Fiberglass has reached new heights in the fiberglass piping industry through its commitment to old-world craftsmanship combined with 21st-century technology.

The Cortinez Law Firm

WHEN ROBERT CORTINEZ ENTERED THE UNITED STATES ARMY, IT WAS AS AN EN-LISTED MAN. HE WORKED HIS WAY UP THE RANKS, BECOMING A PARATROOPER IN THE 101ST AIRBORNE DIVISION—WHICH GUARDED THE SAFETY OF AFRICAN-AMERICAN STUDENTS AT CENTRAL HIGH SCHOOL IN 1957—AND THEN SERVING AS A MEMBER

of the Army Special Forces before eventually retiring as a full colonel.

It was his rise from humble beginnings that shaped Cortinez' approach as he founded his law firm. And today he still looks out for the common man and his legal interests. The Cortinez Law Firm is a firm to which all the citizens of Arkansas can turn in times of legal need. The Cortinez firm specializes in criminal defense, personal injury, product liability, domestic issues, and workers' compensation cases. And each of the six lawyers who—along with 13 support and staff people—make up the team at the Cortinez firm has specialized training in at least one of those fields.

SERVING A BROAD AREA OF THE STATE

Cortinez attended the University of Arkansas on the GI Bill, then stayed in Fayetteville—driving a school bus while his wife, Katherine, taught school full-time—to get his law degree. (Katherine still teaches sociology, psychology, and history at Central High.) Cortinez and a partner then came to Little Rock and hung out their shingle. After several different organizational structures, Cortinez settled into the current six-lawyer setup that allows close personal interaction between attorneys and clients. The firm has three offices—Little Rock, Pine Bluff, and Hot Springs—to better serve a wider cross section of Arkansans.

A FAMILY FIRM

Robert Cortinez Jr. has expanded the firm's expertise as a member of the Sports Lawyers Association. As a sports lawyer, Cortinez Jr. deals with any and all issues for athletes, whether they're high schoolers looking into college choices, college athletes who want to transfer schools, or collegians eyeing a professional career. He also is a listed agent who represents pro athletes in all sorts of negotiations.

The Cortinez Law Firm's commitment to the common man's legal needs has prompted it to take cases that aren't necessarily financially lucrative. "Some firms work only for corporate millionaires," says Robert Cortinez Jr., "but we're a full-service law firm that works by one principle: What's right is right, and what's wrong is wrong." With that view in mind, the Cortinez Law Firm handles many pro bono cases in which they are not paid for their legal services.

Cortinez Jr. works closely with clients referred to him through the Arkansas Enterprises for the Developmentally Disabled, helping assure that the everyday legal problems people find themselves in won't derail these clients in their attempts to forge better lives for themselves.

From the corporate citizen to the common man, the Cortinez Law Firm represents what is good about Little Rock and the state of Arkansas.

Since 1973 the Cortinez Law Firm has served Arkansans from its offices in downtown Little Rock.

▶ MATT BRADLEY

LITTLE ROCK ATHLETIC CLUB

THE EXTENSIVE LIST OF FEATURES AND SERVICES OFFERED BY THE LITTLE ROCK ATHLETIC CLUB HAS MADE IT THE CLUB OF CHOICE IN MEETING THE DIVERSE FITNESS NEEDS OF THE CENTRAL ARKANSAS COMMUNITY. SINCE ITS FOUNDING IN 1973, THE LITTLE ROCK ATHLETIC CLUB HAS FOCUSED ON ONE GOAL—TO CREATE A POSITIVE, NURTURING ENVIRONMENT STRESSING THE mental and physical benefits of leading an active, participatory, and health-conscious lifestyle.

Since its inception as Westside Tennis Club with six indoor courts, tennis has been a primary focus at the facility, which boasts nine indoor courts and four outdoor hard courts. Other racquet sports also are emphasized with four racquetball and one squash court. In addition, the club features an indoor track, a six-lane indoor/outdoor swimming pool, a large gymnasium with basketball and volleyball courts, Cybex, BodyMasters, free-weight equipment, an aerobics studio, and amenities such as massage, sauna, steam room, and whirlpool. To better serve its clients, the club also offers child care facilities, laundry service, men's and women's locker rooms, restaurant, and pro shop.

Little Rock Athletic Club is situated on nine acres in west Little Rock. The club currently includes 120,000 square feet of indoor recreational space. In March 1996 the club completed a 7,000-square-foot children's center that caters to children 14 years old and under, and offers basketball, soccer, volleyball, and an indoor playground with colorful "soft-play" equipment.

The club is staffed by carefully selected fitness professionals who are dedicated to serving the members by coordinating the use of the extensive facilities to promote members' participation and health awareness.

Word-of-mouth referrals have helped the Little Rock Athletic Club grow, a testament to the range of products and services that have helped it become the area's club of choice.

ABOVE: *Little Rock Athletic Club is situated on nine acres in west Little Rock and currently includes 120,000 square feet of indoor recreational space.*

CLOCKWISE FROM NEAR RIGHT: *Since its inception as Westside Tennis Club with six indoor courts, tennis has been a primary focus at the facility, which boasts nine indoor courts and four outdoor hard courts.*

The club features an indoor track, a large gymnasium with basketball and volleyball courts, two separate 3,000-square-foot weight rooms, and many other amenities.

In March 1996 the club completed a 7,000-square-foot children's recreational center that caters to children 14 years old and under.

The club's swimming pool, which has six lanes and is 25 yards long, is enclosed during the winter months by an air-supported structure allowing year-round swimming by club members.

CARTI (CENTRAL ARKANSAS RADIATION THERAPY INSTITUTE)

FOR TWO DECADES CARTI (CENTRAL ARKANSAS RADIATION THERAPY INSTITUTE) HAS MET THE NEEDS OF AREA CANCER PATIENTS. CARTI IS THE ONLY RADIATION THERAPY FACILITY IN LITTLE ROCK, AND SINCE 1976 HAS PROVIDED THE HIGHEST QUALITY CANCER TREATMENT, COMPASSIONATE PATIENT CARE, EDUCATIONAL AND SUPPORT PROGRAMS, AND RESEARCH.

As a not-for-profit facility, CARTI provides treatment, patient services, prevention and educational programs, and follow-up sessions regardless of a patient's ability to pay. Its leading role in quality cancer care has been nationally recognized: CARTI was the first free-standing not-for-profit radiation therapy center ever to receive accreditation from the Joint Commission on Accreditation of Healthcare Organizations in 1989, and has since served as a model to other centers nationwide.

CARTI began in Little Rock as a cooperative effort between Baptist Medical Center, University of Arkansas Medical Center, Veteran's Administration Hospital, and St. Vincent Infirmary Medical Center. CARTI opened its doors in 1976 on the St. Vincent campus in Little Rock, expanding to Searcy in 1988 and Mountain Home in 1989. The CARTI/Conway Regional Cancer Center, a cooperative effort between CARTI and Conway Regional Medical Center, opened in Conway in 1996.

A HISTORY OF HELPING

All area hospitals utilize the services of CARTI for their patients requiring radiation therapy and CARTI has treated more than 43,000 cancer patients since its beginning. CARTI facilities are staffed with board-certified radiation oncologists, certified radiation therapists, radiation physicists, nurses, transport assistants, and other support personnel.

CARTI's counseling and resource coordinators assist patients and their families with counseling, financial resources, cancer education materials, transportation, housing, nutritional information, and home health care services and equipment.

CARTI is committed to Arkansas and its people by providing many free outreach programs. The CancerAnswers® program reaches 13,000 former cancer patients statewide through a quarterly newsletter. Free luncheon/education classes are offered in 12 communities. Celebration of Life events are held around the state to honor CARTI patients and other cancer survivors.

SPECIAL KIDS GET SPECIAL CARE

Kids are special at CARTI. The CARTI Kids are treated to a sum-

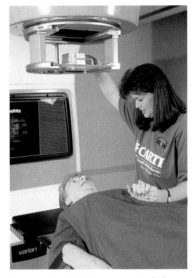

mer weekend retreat and a Christmas party each year. CARTI has developed a school reentry program called Hairballs on My Pillow® and a children's grief and loss program called Drying Their Tears℠. Free screenings and risk-identification educational programs offered by CARTI across the state address the key to a cancer cure—prevention and early diagnosis.

CARTI's Foundation was incorporated in 1983 to assist CARTI in developing and implementing fund-raising programs and, through the investment and use of funds raised, to aid in supporting the cancer treatment and education efforts of CARTI.

As it marks its 20th year of service to the community and the state, CARTI's mission continues compassionate patient care that also encompasses the family, education for patients and the public, and a commitment to funding cancer research.

ABOVE LEFT: *CARTI's services include assistance with transportation, housing, medicine, counseling, and other patient and family needs.*

ABOVE: *CARTI combines compassionate care with state-of-the-art technology to provide the highest quality cancer treatment.*

LEFT: *Since 1977 CARTI Auxiliary's Festival of Trees, a four-day annual holiday fund-raiser, has raised more than $1 million for CARTI programs and services.*

PHOTOGRAPHS BY KELLY QUINN

COLUMBIA HEALTH SYSTEM OF ARKANSAS

OLUMBIA HEALTH SYSTEM OF ARKANSAS BRINGS TO THE STATE A NEW FORM OF MEDICAL CARE THAT IS PAVING THE WAY FOR AN INNOVATIVE APPROACH TO DELIVERING HEALTH CARE TO ARKANSANS. ❧ AS AN AFFILIATE OF COLUMBIA/HCA HEALTHCARE CORPORATION, COLUMBIA HEALTH SYSTEM OF ARKANSAS IS ABLE TO OFFER A CONTINUUM OF QUALITY

health care, cost effectively for the people in the Arkansas communities it serves. Columbia/HCA is the nation's largest provider of health care services, with more than 340 hospitals, 120 outpatient surgery centers, and 250 home health agencies in 38 states, England, and Switzerland. Columbia is building comprehensive networks of health care services, including home health, rehabilitation, and skilled nursing facilities in local markets around the country.

The growing Columbia system in Arkansas includes Columbia Doctors Hospital in Little Rock; Medical Center of South Arkansas in El Dorado; DeQueen Regional Medical Center in DeQueen; Medical Park Hospital in Hope; and four multispecialty clinics.

AN INNOVATIVE APPROACH

Columbia's mission is to work closely with physicians, employees, volunteers, and the community to provide a seamless system of quality health care for the people of Arkansas through its innovative approach to health care.

Employees at each of the medical facilities are working as a team with physicians to assure that quality care is provided. Whether it's an expectant mother ready to enter the hospital, a senior adult visiting a clinic for nutritional counseling, or a child undergoing an eye examination, patients can be assured that quality care will be delivered throughout the Columbia network of employees and volunteers working hand in hand for the same mission.

Columbia Doctors Hospital, a 328-bed major medical center centrally located in Little Rock, has a complete scope of quality health services administered by a dedicated and caring staff of health care professionals. Centers of excellence include a chronic pain management center, the state's leading obstetrics services, a premier hand and microsurgery center, a rehabilitation center, a hip and knee joint

Senior Friends Coordinator Jean Ciampi (left) greets a potential member in front of the Senior Friends office at Columbia Doctors Hospital.

LEFT: *Columbia Doctors Hospital's 24-hour emergency department is open seven days a week.*

BELOW LEFT: *As an affiliate of Columbia/ HCA Healthcare Corporation, Columbia Health System of Arkansas is able to offer a continuum of quality health care, cost effectively for the people in the Arkansas communities it serves.*

replacement center, and a Senior Friends benefit program for persons 50 and over. Columbia and other private-sector organizations are reshaping the health care system in Arkansas and across the country, changing it into one in which providers compete on the basis of quality and efficiency. Columbia is working towards a better tomorrow in health care by making needed changes today.

COMMUNITY SERVICE

Columbia's involvement goes outside its facilities' walls into the community. The organization works hard to be a good corporate citizen as a strong supporter of United Way on a local and national basis, and as a corporate sponsor for such health care organizations as the Susan G. Komen Foundation's Race for the Cure. Its employees work side by side on committees

with other leaders in community charitable organizations such as the American Cancer Society, the American Heart Association, and the Arkansas Arthritis Foundation.

Partnerships with community groups, physicians, health plan providers, and local businesses and industries in Arkansas help posi-

tion Columbia Health System of Arkansas as a leader in health care in the state. The commitment to providing patients with cost-effective quality and compassionate care should ensure this leadership position for years to come.

THE HAGAN AGENCY, INC.

Hospitals have made the Hagan Agency, Inc. healthier than ever. The momentum the company has gained from its strong working relationship with the health care industry in Arkansas has propelled the property and casualty insurance agency into a period of unprecedented growth. ❧ The Hagan Agency's billing

increased from $1.2 million in premiums in 1989 to $20 million in 1994. During those boom years, the independent agency grew from four to 38 employees, and went from selling the products and services of five major insurance companies to more than 20. In 1991 the Arkansas Hospital Association made the Hagan Agency its only recommended provider for Arkansas hospitals.

Today the agency's expertise in providing insurance for hospitals is fueling the major portion of the company's growth. Hagan now services 27 of the 126 hospitals in Arkansas, and the firm is adding more clients all the time.

A LOOK BACK

The Hagan Agency was founded December 31, 1979, by Calvin E. Hagan, who had been Arkansas manager of Southland Life Insurance Co. for 16 years. The company remained strictly a life insurance agency for its first five years, but a merger in 1984 with a 35-year-old property and casualty insurance agency changed the company's focus.

A second major move occurred in 1989 when Calvin Hagan and his son, Bubba, formed Hagan-Newkirk Financial Services, which structures employee benefit packages and also specializes in working with hospitals. With the formation

of Hagan-Newkirk, Debbie Hagan-Sherwin, Calvin's daughter, remained as the only Hagan family member working full-time at the Hagan Agency, where she now is president. The complementary relationship between the two companies has proven successful in servicing the health care industry's total insurance needs.

In 1990 the Hagan Agency expanded its commercial insurance department and laid the groundwork for its strong position with hospitals in Arkansas through the hiring of three experienced agents with successful backgrounds in hospital insurance; two more came on board in the following years.

RIGHT: *Since 1989, through successful employee training and a strategy aimed toward growth, the Hagan Agency has grown from four to 38 employees and from selling the products and services of five major insurance companies to more than 20.*

PHOTOGRAPHY BY CUNNINGHAM PHOTOGRAPHY

LEFT: *To Calvin Hagan and Hagan Agency President Debbie Hagan-Sherwin a satisfied client is the best indicator of success.*

The addition of five agents with decades of proven expertise in commercial insurance became the springboard for the Hagan Agency's phenomenal growth in the first half of the 1990s.

The Hagan Agency has a six-person Medical Department trained in every facet of medical professional liability and health care services insurance. The department processes and services the agency's many hospital accounts. Together, the six agents have more than 175 years' experience in the insurance business.

SERVICE STRESSED

In all its work, the Hagan Agency stresses service, including a claims office, open 24 hours a day. When a policy is written and delivered to a client, it always includes a policy review to ensure the policy is complete.

Another component to the firm's service involves agent education. Dramatic changes in both the insurance industry and the health care industry require that Hagan Agency agents regularly attend continuing education classes as well as the most advanced seminars and conferences on health care. It is their aim to not only keep up with all the changes but to stay ahead of the trends.

As an independent insurance agency, the Hagan Agency works with more than 20 nationally recognized insurance companies across the nation, allowing Hagan agents to shop for a wider variety of policies in order to fit the precise needs of their clients. It also allows them to offer the most competitive prices available in the market.

HAPPY CUSTOMERS

To Debbie Hagan-Sherwin, a satisfied client is the best indicator of her company's success. In fact, she proudly points to a list of Hagan customers that reads like a who's who of Arkansas business leaders. The list includes Baptist Health, Baldwin & Shell Construction Company, Coy's Steak House, Andy's Restaurants, Jr. Food Mart of Arkansas, Ouachita Baptist University, Munsey Products, Rector-Phillips-Morse, Inc., Ranger Boats, and the Texas League's Arkansas Travelers.

According to Debbie Hagan-Sherwin, that commercial client list keeps growing in size and status. And it is her hope that the agency's aggressive effort to build upon its working relationship with commercial customers in Arkansas will help ensure the last half of the 1990s will be as historically significant for the Hagan Agency as the first half.

THE JANET JONES COMPANY

THE JANET JONES COMPANY IS SOLD ON LITTLE ROCK. AND THAT MESSAGE COMES ACROSS LOUD AND CLEAR AS ITS 28 AGENTS WORK TO HELP CUSTOMERS FIND A PLACE IN THE COMMUNITY—A HOME, NOT MERELY A HOUSE. ❧ JONES AND HER HUSBAND, LELAND "BUD" JONES, FOUNDED THE COMPANY IN 1980, OPENING FOR BUSINESS WITH A SIMPLE PHILOSOPHY: TREAT EVERYONE AS you would like to be treated.

That service-oriented credo has remained a constant, even as the company has grown markedly, from one agent to 28 with a support staff of eight.

BUILDING RELATIONSHIPS

Years ago, the telephone rang at The Janet Jones Company office and the caller posed a fairly unusual question. "I have an antique lace bedspread that was my grand-mother's. Where should I take it to be dry-cleaned?" The agents on duty quickly pooled their collective knowledge of the area dry cleaners and made a suggestion. Another caller wanted to know which university sorority sold pecans during the holidays. Both of the people who called the real estate office for answers to these decidedly non-real estate questions said they "just knew" they'd get their answers.

Indeed, building the sorts of relationships that spawn such phone calls is at the heart of what has made The Janet Jones Company a major player in the Little Rock real estate market. A sense of family creates a supportive atmosphere within the agency and the strong relationships inside the office contribute to the tight customer/agent bonds the company regularly forms. Janet Jones agents know they are likely to be the first friends

The Janet Jones Company is sold on Little Rock and that message comes across loud and clear as its 28 agents work to help customers find a place in the community—a home, not merely a house.

▼ BILL PARSONS

a potential home buyer will have when that person or family comes to Little Rock, and the company takes that responsibility and challenge very seriously.

SELLING LITTLE ROCK

As Little Rock has grown, The Janet Jones Company has also expanded its market area. Agents actively list and sell property in Little Rock, Maumelle, Cabot, Sherwood, Jacksonville, North Little Rock, and all of Saline County. The company's primary focus, however, remains on the area loosely defined as west Little Rock—from the bottom of Cantrell Hill, west to the Perry County line, south of the river, and north of Interstate 630. The firm is the leading real estate agency in the prestigious Heights and Hillcrest areas, as well as in the midtown neighborhoods of Foxcroft, Leawood, Robinwood, River Ridge, and Pleasant Valley, and ranks high in other growing parts of town, including Longlea, Chenal Valley, Chenal Parkway, West Markham, and Hinson Road.

Janet Jones Company agents are experts on Little Rock and are among the city's most active advocates. The company has formed many partnerships within the business community to encourage prospective employees to relocate to Little Rock.

As a recognized leader in relocation and a member of the prestigious RELO network, The Janet Jones Company has introduced hundreds of families to the community. Agents working with the Janet Jones relocation department often tour the city with people even before they've decided whether they'll move to Little Rock. And the relocation effort goes both ways. Customers who are considering a move to another city can call on The Janet Jones Company to supply information about homes—and a full community profile—across the country and even abroad.

▶ MATT BRADLEY

Janet Jones and her husband, Leland "Bud" Jones, founded The Janet Jones Company, opening for business with a simple philosophy: Treat everyone as you would like to be treated.

IN TOUCH WITH THE COMMUNITY

As part of their commitment to offering customers a full range of services and knowledge, Janet Jones agents work through a variety of community projects to keep up with all that's going on in the area. Agents are active in area churches and are volunteers in both public and private schools, the Little Rock Chamber of Commerce, and the Board of Realtors, as well as numerous other community organizations.

The decision to use the rainbow as the company logo was not a frivolous one. The rainbow represents hope for the future, which is reflected by The Janet Jones Company's optimism, enthusiasm, positive approach to problem solving, and dedication to impeccable service. Treating customers like family, selling Little Rock as enthusiastically as the city's beautiful homes, giving back to the community through service work: All of these things explain why Janet Jones agents often say, "Selling houses is just a small part of what we do."

Ramsey, Krug, Farrell & Lensing, Inc.

Sixteen years after they banded together to form an insurance agency, Tad Krug, Tim Farrell, and Ron Lensing are still at the heart of the organization. That much has remained the same. But the three men have surrounded themselves with more than 50 professionals, who over the years have helped their firm—Ramsey, Krug,

Farrell & Lensing, Inc.—exponentially expand its line of products and services to meet the changing needs of its client base.

Growth has demanded greater specialization and continued education for all the agents at Ramsey, Krug, Farrell & Lensing. Although the firm does business in all 50 states and every province in Canada, its primary service area continues to be Arkansas. "Our mission is to plan and buy asset protection for our clients with service that exceeds their expectations," says Krug, chairman of the company.

Founded in 1980 after Thomas T. Ramsey, Krug, and Farrell sold an earlier insurance firm, the Little Rock-based agency has retained Ramsey's name in its title in honor of the retired partner, now deceased.

RIGHT: *The three founders of Ramsey, Krug, Farrell & Lensing—(from left) Tad Krug, CIC; Ron Lensing, CIC; and Tim Farrell, CIC—have guided the firm since 1980.*

BELOW RIGHT: *Working together in a spirit of adaptability helps separate the Ramsey, Krug, Farrell & Lensing staff from its competitors.*

there in the middle of the night," Krug says. "That's when people are the most anxious for results." Thus, the company motto: "When lightning strikes, we strike back."

Ramsey, Krug, Farrell &

24-Hour Claims Service

The primary service Ramsey, Krug, Farrell & Lensing offers is its ability to respond quickly and effectively when a client has a claim. The company provides 24-hour claim reporting services, seven days a week. "If a tornado hits your home, we'll get a restoration company

Lensing has developed three areas of specialization in the insurance field: professional liability, construction/surety, and transportation. While business insurance is still the primary focus at Ramsey, Krug, Farrell & Lensing, the firm also places a strong emphasis on risk-management services through

a subsidiary—Risk Management Resources (RMR).

RMR provides risk management services for larger clients and groups, as well as claims services, administered across the United States and Canada in an equipment dealer program that currently serves more than 1,500 dealers.

Continued Growth

Indeed, growth and specialization have been a way of life at Ramsey, Krug, Farrell & Lensing since its founding. And that's not about to change. The agency has almost outgrown its headquarters in the center of Little Rock and will be eyeing relocation or expansion as it continues to tailor programs to fit the needs of its clients. That spirit of adaptability is what helps separate the firm from its competitors.

"We want to custom-design a program with our client that fits their needs—a program that will be unique and will work for all parties involved," Krug adds. "We're trying to attract clients who want us to serve their needs for a long-term relationship, not just to sell them an insurance policy."

Magic 105 and K-Duck 100

W ITH ITS PURCHASE OF MAGIC 105 AND K-DUCK 100 IN 1996, CLEAR CHANNEL COMMUNICATIONS INSTANTLY BECAME A MAJOR PLAYER IN THE CENTRAL ARKANSAS RADIO MARKET. MAGIC 105 (KMJX-FM) HAS BEEN THE AREA'S CLEAR LEADER IN CLASSIC ROCK PROGRAMMING SINCE ITS FOUNDING IN 1980, WHILE K-DUCK

(KDDK-FM) burst on the scene in 1992 with more new country music than listeners here had ever been offered.

The two stations rank third and fourth, respectively, in cumulative audience, together drawing more than 158,000 listeners—giving them a secure foothold with two of the most popular styles of music. Owned until 1996 by U.S. Radio, the stations were purchased by Clear Channel, a San Antonio, Texas-based company.

BEAT GOES ON AT MAGIC 105
Album-oriented rock and roll (AOR) has been the name of the game at Magic 105 since day one. That consistency has helped the station achieve solid, steady growth over the years and to develop a loyal au-

dience. In a business where change is constant, Magic 105 has stayed the course: Of all the FM stations on the air when Magic 105 debuted, all but one has had at least one change in format in addition to significant changes in on-air personalities.

Widely known and wildly popular, Tommy "The Outlaw" Smith has kept his morning drive-time audiences entertained—both comically and musically—since the station's founding. Following The Outlaw each morning is another familiar voice, Tom Wood, who has been program director at Magic

105 since day one. He hosts the *Brownbagger*, an all-request lunch-hour show that has become so popular it has even spawned a theme song, "Brownbag Blues."

GETTING ITS DUCKS IN A ROW
Many stations had tried to compete against KSSN, the country music giant that perennially is the area's top-rated station. But none had succeeded until K-Duck 100. The ratings have been strong for KDDK-FM since it hit the air in July 1992 with an attention-grabbing personality, the Duck, who makes frequent promotional ap-

pearances. K-Duck 100's niche has always been new country, that brand of country music that has rocketed in popularity since 1990. The station hooked listeners with long stretches of uninterrupted country music and still capitalizes on that appeal with its slogan: "Nobody plays more country."

Both Magic 105 and K-Duck 100 have been active in the community from the beginning. Magic 105's annual Living Billboard campaign has been a strong fund-raiser for the American Cancer Society and a real source of talk around town as drivers spot station personalities perched atop a billboard. K-Duck 100's Rubber Ducky Regatta—a natural tie-in—is held each year at Wild River Country and also benefits the American Cancer Society. Employees of both stations also are active in Red Cross blood drives, and Magic 105 broadcasts a one-hour public-affairs show each Sunday morning.

ABOVE: *With the American Cancer Society as the recipient, Magic 105's Living Billboard demonstrates the station's commitment to its community.*

FAR LEFT: *Broadcasting live from Showcase '96, K-Duck 100's Kevin King gets some assistance from K-Duck.*

NEAR LEFT: *Radio personalities Tommy "The Outlaw" Smith and Big Dave rustle up the best breakfast in Little Rock.*

JONES PRODUCTIONS, INC.

GARY JONES HAS A PASSION FOR QUALITY AND CREATIVITY THAT HAS MADE JONES PRODUCTIONS, INC. (JPI) ONE OF MID-AMERICA'S PREMIER MOTION PICTURE AND TELEVISION RESOURCES. ✌ "WE COMBINE ART AND TECHNOLOGY ON BEHALF OF BUSINESSES REQUIRING HIGH-END TELEVISION COMMERCIALS AND CORPORATE VIDEOS," JONES OBSERVES.

As the energizer of the Arkansas production community, Jones has more than three decades of filmmaking experience, a master's degree in television, and management credentials with leading communication companies in the United States and Canada.

Jones Productions, Inc., founded in 1981, is in downtown Little Rock. JPI is home to a fiber-optics-connected studio; a state-of-the-art, digital-component post-production suite; a leading-edge computer animation service; the region's first nonlinear editing facil-

BOTTOM LEFT: Jones Productions' D5 post and compositing suite is unsurpassed for speed and quality.

BOTTOM RIGHT: Jones Film & Video has the only "drive-in" soundstage in the downtown Little Rock area.

ity; and two 35mm camera systems supported by three-ton and five-ton grip and lighting trucks.

A VARIETY OF FORMATS

Gary Jones is the region's only accredited IMAX® filmmaker. He photographed and edited the signature film "Arkansas: Center of Attraction," which shows daily at the Aerospace Education Center in Little Rock. "Large-format cinematography is very demanding and equally rewarding," he says. "When your efforts fill a screen six stories high, you need a keen eye for detail. And with the 85-pound IMAX

them to accept nothing less than the best from themselves on each project."

ADVANCED TECHNOLOGY

Jones Film & Video has a legacy of production firsts in the region. Among the latest examples of innovation and leadership, JF&V was the first facility in the area to install a completely transparent, 100 percent uncompressed, D5 digital component production environment, which assures that no details in a frame are lost. JF&V specialties include flawless multilayer video compositing and blue-screen special

cameras, my crew and I also need strong backs."

Although Jones Film & Video (JF&V), a division of Jones Productions, Inc., has produced two feature films, the majority of its 35mm projects are award-winning commercials for regional advertising agencies. "We serve the client wanting a $150,000 network-quality film commercial for $50,000," says Rex W. Jones, director of operations. "We don't cut corners and we don't resort to smoke and mirrors. What we do is invest heavily in good equipment and great people. Then we challenge

effects. The highest-quality technology is employed in these processes to guarantee the cleanest, most realistic effects for viewer enjoyment.

Jones Film & Video was the first production company in the region to utilize the speed of computer editing. Using the most advanced computer systems available, JF&V editors lead the way with speed and creativity in nonlinear editing.

Electric Ink™, the company's three-dimensional computer animation service, offers the most sophisticated graphics in the market. Using feature-film-quality worksta-

LEFT: *Jones Productions owns two 35mm film camera systems and is one of the most experienced motion picture companies in Arkansas.*

CLOCKWISE FROM BELOW: *JPI Founder Gary W. Jones has been an award-winning director/cinematographer since 1963.*

Jones Productions computer artists use Softimage and other world-class graphics software.

Electric Ink™ is Jones Productions' subsidiary for creating high-end 3D animation and graphics.

The Jones Productions Center at 517 Chester near the Arkansas State Capitol has been serving mid-America producers since 1981.

tions and software, the company's digital magicians provide high-end animation for clients throughout the United States.

Jones Film & Video is a full-service production company working in creative partnership with leading advertising agencies. "Advertising agencies are under a lot of pressure and are undergoing a lot of change. We try to make their jobs easier by helping them deliver top-quality, top-value productions to their clients," Gary Jones says.

TEAM JPI

Jones Productions, Inc. also has staff writers and producers to handle turnkey creative assignments from script-to-screen (or more likely from script-to-massive-amounts-of-VHS-copies-that-have-to-go-out-tomorrow). "Companies are relying more and more on video to communicate to customers, stockholders, and employees," Rex Jones notes. "There is tremendous growth in top-quality corporate and institutional video. It's the best way for busy executives to leverage limited time for maximum impact."

"Film is a collaborative medium. It always has been," Gary Jones says. "It takes a creative group of

people with the right tools and technical skills to produce a great 30-second commercial. We've been doing this successfully for a long time. It's a wonderful job. I don't ever plan to retire because I'm having too much fun."

"The Team JPI concept," says Rex Jones, "is not some abstract

theory to us. It's a daily reality. It's a commitment to our clients and to ourselves for mutual support in the quest to be the best. As individuals, we can appreciate perfection; only as a team can we achieve it."

TCBY Enterprises, Inc.

TCBY Enterprises, Inc. has always found new ways to treat its customers since the day in September 1981 when the first store opened in the Market Place shopping center on Rodney Parham Road. At first it was simply with soft-serve frozen yogurt, a new concept in frozen desserts that led founder Frank Hickingbotham to proclaim,

"This can't be yogurt."

Today the aptly named TCBY Treats stores still serve the high-quality soft-serve frozen yogurt products known by everyone, while also offering a variety of other dessert items, encouraging new customers to visit the stores and existing customers to visit more frequently. The Treats concept was introduced in 1995 and immediately generated tremendous interest from consumers and franchisees excited about the expanded offerings of TCBY hand-dipped frozen yogurt and TCBY premium ice cream, available in 16 flavors.

A second area of emphasis for TCBY is a strategy through which TCBY products are offered through operators in nontraditional locations such as airports, educational facilities, hospitals, travel plazas, convenience stores, hotels, stadiums, and theme parks—more than 1,300 in all.

Marriott is the largest operator of nontraditional TCBY locations. Petroleum company convenience stores owned by Exxon, Mobil, Texaco, and Chevron have enjoyed beneficial co-branding with TCBY, placing it beside such nationally prominent restaurants as McDonald's, Subway, Taco Bell, Arby's, Pizza Hut, Burger King, and Blimpie.

Innovation a Standard

Innovative ways to market innovative products have been a hallmark at TCBY since that fateful day in 1981 in a Dallas shopping mall when Hickingbotham's wife, Georgia, got him to first try frozen yogurt. And when the confirmed yogurt hater loved it, the idea for a business was born. That first store in west Little Rock opened with a simple idea—to provide delicious frozen yogurt products served by friendly people in a clean, wholesome environment. Hickingbotham capitalized on a trend and introduced his products at a time when consumers were becoming keenly aware of eating nutritious foods and maintaining a healthy lifestyle.

Hickingbotham's sons, Herren and Todd, jumped into the middle of the project with their dad, as did a dedicated team of part-time workers, many of whom have gone on to executive positions within the corporation. Quickly it became clear that Frank Hickingbotham's decision to market frozen yogurt as an entity unto itself, rather than have it become lost among the sal-

MARK MATHEWS / PEERLESS PHOTOGRAPHY

ABOVE LEFT AND RIGHT: TCBY's efforts to maintain a high level of brand awareness for TCBY led to the distribution of TCBY frozen hard-pack and refrigerated yogurt in the grocery trade.

RIGHT: Today's TCBY Treats stores serve the high-quality soft-serve frozen yogurt products known by everyone and a variety of other dessert items.

TONY BENNETT PHOTOGRAPHY

ads and sandwiches of health food shops, was right on target.

By the end of the first year, "This Can't Be Yogurt!" had seven corporate stores. People continually asked the Hickingbothams about franchising opportunities, and in 1982 the first franchised stores began to open. In 1983 the watershed marketing slogan "All the Pleasure. None of the Guilt." was introduced. In May 1984, TCBY became a publicly held company, just two and a half years after its first store opened and just five months before its 100th.

TCBY changed its name from This Can't Be Yogurt! to The Country's Best Yogurt in 1984, realizing that—primarily through its success—yogurt had lost its negative image and a "cute" approach was no longer needed. Meanwhile, the staggering growth continued, and the nation's business community took notice. In 1986 and 1987, *Nation's Restaurant News* ranked TCBY first in growth and profitability among 90 publicly owned companies in the food service industry. *Financial World* named TCBY in 1988 as the country's fourth-fastest-growing company. By the end of that year, the company's famed soft-serve yogurt was being served in 1,175 TCBY stores in 49 states and Canada, the Bahamas, and Taiwan.

New challenges came in the early 1990s, as increased competition for traditional frozen yogurt shops, the foundation of TCBY's business, was felt. During this period, the company worked to maintain a high level of brand awareness for TCBY and pursued new avenues of distribution for TCBY products while at the same time pursuing growth opportunities for its franchise system. That led to the distribution of TCBY frozen hard-pack and refrigerated yogurt in the grocery trade and an expansion of the TCBY brand, which now is being served in more than 30 foreign countries. In all, TCBY products are sold in more than 2,700 loca-

tions and the company is the largest manufacturer-franchisor of frozen yogurt in the world.

FROM THE SOURCE

Americana Foods, a wholly owned subsidiary of TCBY, develops and manufactures the company's frozen yogurt and ice cream products in its more than 200,000-square-foot

facility in Dallas. Americana Foods has evolved right along with TCBY stores. The facility originally had the sole purpose of supplying traditional TCBY stores with soft-serve yogurt mix. With the addition of TCBY novelty items to the stores' menus, the plant was expanded to produce those, too. The expansion into novelties also allowed Americana Foods to seek other private-label clients on a larger scale. TCBY's move into the retail grocery trade with hard-pack products required further expansion at Americana to adequately supply those products, as did the implementation of the TCBY Treats concept with its new menu items.

TCBY's Riverport Equipment and Distribution Company and AIMCO provide important services to their customers. These subsidiar-

ies, located in Little Rock, supply all the necessary equipment and fixtures for TCBY stores, as well as other restaurant operations. Together, they offer convenient one-stop shopping for the food service industry.

The innovations TCBY has made in its product line, its delivery methods, its co-branding, and its expansions into nontraditional and foreign markets have helped the company reposition itself in a world of competition that a unique, skillfully marketed concept inevitably creates. The winds of change are powerful, but through flexibility, innovation, and a time-tested standard of excellence, TCBY will continue to diligently pursue its original goal—to serve the world the very best in frozen treats.

CLOCKWISE FROM ABOVE: *TCBY products are being served in more than 30 foreign countries and more than 2,700 locations, making the company the largest manufacturer-franchisor of frozen yogurt in the world.*

TCBY's Riverport Equipment and Distribution Company and AIMCO subsidiaries, located in Little Rock, supply all the necessary equipment and fixtures for TCBY stores, as well as other restaurant operations.

Nontraditional locations and co-branding have placed TCBY in a variety of locations nationwide.

▶ JOHNNY WAITS PHOTOGRAPHY

▶ MARK MATHEWS / PEERLESS PHOTOGRAPHY

▶ MARK MATHEWS / PEERLESS PHOTOGRAPHY

THE CHARLOTTE JOHN COMPANY

SINCE ITS FOUNDING IN 1982, THE CHARLOTTE JOHN COMPANY HAS SPECIALIZED IN LISTING AND SELLING HOMES FROM HILLCREST TO THE WESTERN EDGE OF LITTLE ROCK—PRIME TERRITORY FOR TOP-OF-THE-LINE HOMES AND TOP RESALE VALUES. SINCE THIS IS ALSO THE AREA THAT CHARLOTTE JOHN'S AGENTS CALL HOME, THEY TREAT THEIR CUSTOMERS LIKE

neighbors because that's what they want their customers to become—literally.

While the average Little Rock home sells for about $90,000, homes listed or sold by Charlotte John's team generally run in the $135,000 to $600,000 range—quality houses anyone would be proud to call home.

QUALITY SERVICE: A CREDO

The same quality the Charlotte John agents promote in homes carries over to the service they provide. A midsize sales staff of around 20 people assures that each one is personally familiar with every home the company lists. When you work with one of the friendly Charlotte John agents, you're working with the whole team.

And that includes founder Charlotte John, whose decision to maintain a midsize operation allows her to have a close relationship with all the company's agents and their customers. She may even personally answer the telephone, because she prefers an agent or herself to have initial contact with cli-

ents, putting them at ease rather than routing their calls through a receptionist or voice mail system. This hands-on approach is one of the success secrets John initiated when she struck out on her own after seven years at two larger Little Rock real estate companies.

A PIONEER IN REAL ESTATE CHANGES

Quality service has always been the primary concern of the Charlotte John Company. The company keeps overhead low and commission rates below market to benefit home buyers and sellers. Its innovations in the Little Rock real estate arena have resulted in a win-win situation for all parties involved in transactions with the Charlotte John Company.

From the start, John was convinced that home sellers deserved a lower commission rate. She established a sales commission of 6 percent as the rate for any home her company listed—a full percentage point lower than the advertised rate of her competitors.

John also believes strongly

in a multiple-listing arrangement whereby other companies can show customers her listings and vice versa. She helped pioneer the concept in Little Rock and has remained its strong backer by paying co-brokers a generous share of the commission.

In keeping with its quality goals, technology is one area in which the company has chosen to invest. New computer links allow agents to become familiar with every home on the market. And the Internet makes the communication two-way, as computer users around the world can tap in to see and learn about Little Rock listings. Taking the high-tech approach to today's market, Charlotte John agents have laptop computers, cellular phones, and pagers to remain informed and in touch.

The latest technology is just one more way accessibility and personalized service are guaranteed at the Charlotte John Company—where quality houses, great service, and low commission rates combine to spell success.

RIGHT: *When you work with one of the friendly Charlotte John agents, you're working with the whole team.*

ABOVE: *Company founder Charlotte John, who maintains a close relationship with all the company's agents and their customers, may even personally answer the office telephone.*

PHOTOGRAPHY BY GREER LILE

Arkansas' Excelsior Hotel

Much of what makes Little Rock's Excelsior Hotel what it is lies in where it is. The Excelsior is located in the hub of downtown, along the banks of the Arkansas River, and next to the historic Old State House—where a victorious Bill Clinton made his 1992 election-night presidential acceptance speech.

Only 10 minutes from the airport, the 417-room 20-story luxury hotel offers business travelers and vacationers alike every amenity needed to enjoy a visit to Little Rock.

Something for Everyone

The Excelsior's 21 suites range from simple floor plans to the 3,000-square-foot President Clinton suite. The hotel has four concierge floors—the 16th through the 19th—where guests are provided an independent, separate check-in line; a coffeemaker and terry cloth robe in their room; and exclusive use of the concierge salon, including its complimentary breakfast and its evening hors d'oeuvres service. All concierge rooms have been recently renovated with the business traveler in mind. Among the new innovations is a state-of-the-art telephone system that enables guests to simultaneously connect a modem and maintain voice communications.

Excelsior guests have several dining options, including the heralded Josephine's Library Restaurant, an intimate setting in which to enjoy haute cuisine. The fixed-price menu allows business travelers to predetermine costs when entertaining clients, and the innovative menu is changed weekly. The American Automobile Association proudly cites Josephine's as one of its elite four-diamond award winners.

More casual dining options are available at the Excelsior, as well. Deli on the River features New York-style deli sandwiches; the Apple Blossom, located in the hotel's lobby, offers daily breakfast and lunch service, and a lavish Sunday brunch, complete with live entertainment; and Profiles allows guests to choose from an eclectic menu highlighted by creative salads and pasta dishes. When catered meals are needed, the Excelsior is ready with the services of the largest catering department in the state of Arkansas and a commitment to dining excellence.

A Place for Business

When it is time for business, the Excelsior has plenty to offer. A total of 34 meeting and entertaining rooms of varying sizes and more than 130,000 square feet of event space under one roof include a facility that currently can seat 7,000 people theater-style. A planned 1998 expansion will increase its seating capacity to 12,000. The most recent addition to the Excelsior's event and entertainment space is Josephine's River Ballroom and Terrace. Its elegant ambience and river view make it an excellent choice for upscale events. The Pinnacle Penthouse atop the Excelsior—with its panoramic view of the Arkansas River and downtown Little Rock—is the perfect place for private parties for up to 200.

The luxury at the Excelsior brings with it a full range of services, including a high-tech fitness center provided complimentarily for guests, newsstand, florist, gift shop, one-day laundry and dry-cleaning service, room service, baby-sitters, a house physician on call, and an arts-and-crafts store.

For visitors seeing the hometown of a president, or for business travelers, every guest of the Excelsior Hotel receives the finest service possible. Time spent at the Excelsior is memorable for all the right reasons. Something important happens every day at the Excelsior!

Only 10 minutes from the airport, the 417-room 20-story Arkansas' Excelsior Hotel offers business travelers and vacationers alike every amenity needed to enjoy a visit to Little Rock.

MOLEX INC.

*N*OWHERE IS THE DYNAMIC GROWTH OF MOLEX INC. MORE APPARENT THAN AT ITS MAUMELLE MANUFACTURING FACILITY. THE LISLE, ILLINOIS-BASED MANUFACTURER OF ELECTRONIC CONNECTORS CAME TO ARKANSAS IN 1984 WITH A DOZEN EMPLOYEES AND A 38,000-SQUARE-FOOT FACILITY. NINE YEARS LATER THE PLANT MORE THAN QUADRUPLED IN SIZE,

and today its approximately 550 employees are already looking toward future expansion possibilities.

General Manager Dennis Williams attributes the dramatic increase in size to the growth in the professional electronics industry. A member of Molex's DataComm division, the Maumelle plant produces connectors that link electronic components in equipment for industry heavyweights such as IBM, Hewlett-Packard, Compaq, and Intel.

Improvements in quality have been fostered through the plant's commitment to total quality management, which empowers workers

RIGHT: Molex manufactures approximately 50,000 products, which are offered through a network of direct sales, distribution, and manufacturers' representatives.

BELOW: Molex, the Lisle, Illinois-based manufacturer of electronic connectors, came to Arkansas in 1984.

to make crucial on-line decisions and thus take more ownership in the manufacturing process. The Maumelle plant features injection molding, high-speed stamping, reel-to-reel electroplating, and automated assembly.

FROM FLOWERPOTS TO ELECTRICAL CONNECTORS

Doing business worldwide wasn't even a dream of Frederick A. Krehbiel's when he invented the black, gunky plastic material called Molex in 1938. He was happy to

simply sell his invention for use in making flowerpots, toy guns, and saltshakers.

Krehbiel and his son John H. Krehbiel Jr., who is the current president of the company, found through their tinkering that Molex had exceptional electrical conducting capacities. And when the use of other plastics was restricted during World War II, manufacturers turned to Molex as a substitute. After the war, Molex entered the electrical appliance market, and in the 1950s and 1960s began producing pin and socket connectors for Magnavox, Zenith, and RCA to link electronic components in color television sets.

The big year for Molex came in 1967, when John sent his son Frederick Krehbiel II to Japan to sell his company's connectors to the many television manufacturers there. To say the rest is history would be understating things. Today Molex generates more than 70 percent of its sales overseas with 44 plants in 21 countries, all with native management teams.

Molex manufactures approximately 50,000 products, which are

offered through a network of direct sales, distribution, and manufacturers' representatives. Primary products include electronic, electrical, and fiber-optic connection systems; ribbon cable; switches; and application tooling. Employing more than 9,500 people, Molex has captured 5.3 percent of the estimated $22.4 billion electronic connector market—making it the second-largest connector manufacturer in the world. Molex is traded on the NASDAQ national market system in the United States and on the London Stock Exchange.

"If you are going to survive in today's global economy," Krehbiel II says, "you have to be where your customers are. You have to listen to your customers and make what they want, the way they want it."

Around the world, Molex employees work to serve a variety of customers. In the process, they're building a larger, more efficient team.

Lynda Bowers & Associates, Realtors

FOR THE PAST 21 YEARS LYNDA BOWERS HAS CONTINUOUSLY BEEN ONE OF THE MOST SUCCESSFUL REALTORS IN THE GREATER LITTLE ROCK AREA. SINCE FOUNDING HER OWN COMPANY IN 1986 WITH ONLY ONE OTHER AGENT AND AN OFFICE ADMINISTRATOR, HER FIRM HAS GROWN TO A TEAM OF 12 DEDICATED AND EXPERIENCED PROFESSIONALS WHOSE COMMITMENT TO SERVICE GOES

beyond helping clients find the best possible home in the best possible area for the best possible price. "Lynda Bowers & Associates delivers a variety of services that make buying or selling a home easier," says Bowers, "including property management, leasing, and relocation services."

SPECIALIZED SERVICES
Bowers emphasizes that her firm specializes in residential real estate

and relocation services and handles properties in all price ranges and all areas of Greater Little Rock, including Maumelle, North Little Rock, Sherwood, Benton, and Cabot. "Our associates are very knowledgeable about the central Arkansas market and through our affiliation with CARMLS we have access to every home listed in the area," says Bowers.

Associate Broker Sharon Brent, a nationally recognized relocation director, works closely with incoming and outbound clients who are referred to the appropriate agent or, when leaving Little Rock, to the best out-of-town company. Brent is one of only two real estate agents

in Arkansas who are members of the Relocation Directors Council, a group highly selective in its membership. "Through our affiliation with the Employee Relocation Council [ERC] we work with companies to help their employees find the right house and feel at home when they move into the area," says Brent. The ERC is made up of Fortune 500 companies, relocation directors, real estate brokers, appraisers, and third-party companies.

A COMMUNITY ROLE
Bowers' commitment to honesty and integrity in real estate transactions extends beyond the company. "One of our strengths is that so many of our agents are community minded and work with local organizations to make Greater Little Rock a better place to live," says Bowers, who currently serves as vice president of the Maumelle Chamber of Commerce and as a member of the Little Rock Metro Rotary Club, Better Business Bureau Board of Directors, and Pulaski County Schools Budget

Advisory Committee.

In addition to sponsoring a voter registration booth at the annual Maumelle Fourth of July Celebration for the past 10 years, the company sponsors baseball, softball, basketball, and soccer teams and participates in fund-raising events for Arkansas Easter Seals, United Cerebral Palsy, Maumelle Friends of the Animals, and North Little Rock Boys Club. An annual landscape fair and garden show the company has put on for years has evolved into a full-fledged outdoor exposition showcasing area nurseries, landscape and lawn services, pool and pest control businesses, florist shops, and the Pulaski County Extension Department.

The company's dedicated associates and the extra services they offer have made a big difference for many families living in and relocating to the Greater Little Rock area. "Much of our business comes from repeat customers and referrals," says Bowers, "and many of our agents and customers become good friends."

FAR LEFT: *Lynda Bowers & Associates, Realtors delivers a variety of services that make buying or selling a home easier, including property management, leasing, and relocation services.*

BELOW: *Since founding her own company in 1986, Lynda Bowers has encouraged her team of dedicated and experienced professionals to help clients find the best possible home in the best possible area for the best possible price.*

COURTYARD BY MARRIOTT

DESIGNED BY BUSINESS TRAVELERS FOR BUSINESS TRAVELERS—COURTYARD BY MARRIOTT'S CORPORATE SLOGAN IS EVIDENT IN EVERY DETAIL. THE 149-ROOM HOTEL BUILT IN WEST LITTLE ROCK IN 1988 OFFERS A COMPREHENSIVE COMBINATION OF AMENITIES AND SERVICES TO HELP BUSINESS TRAVELERS GET THEIR WORK DONE, THEN ENJOY THEIR LEISURE

time. Located just seconds from the intersection of Interstates 430 and 630—quickly becoming the center of business activity in Little Rock—the Courtyard is convenient to travelers coming from or working in any direction. Each room at the

Courtyard is an office and living room rolled into one. Work desks are included in all rooms, and the telephones allow guests to hook up computers directly to receive or transmit information by modem. With the in-room voice mail system, guests can retrieve telephone messages and set their own wake-up calls.

Each guest room includes a seating area. Coffee and tea are available in all rooms, and suites also include a dry bar and refrigerator. Balconies on interior rooms face toward the courtyard and include patio furniture. The outdoor swimming pool area is lined with chairs and chaise lounges and has a gazebo nearby that offers a break from the sun. Indoors is a whirlpool large enough to accommodate eight to 10 guests, accented by a large skylight.

BUSINESS CENTER FOR GUESTS

The commitment to convenience for business travelers extends outside the guest rooms, too. The Courtyard's front desk operates as a business center for guests, with copying and fax service available. There are two conference rooms for larger meetings, each capable of accommodating groups of 50. The hotel works with local caterers to provide meals, or clients can arrange their own service if they choose.

The Courtyard's exercise facility offers health-conscious guests many workout options—a treadmill, stair stepper, universal weight machine, and exercise bike. A television mounted in the corner gives exercisers a mental break from their routines. Exercise room hours are 6 a.m. to 11 p.m. but can be customized to fit guests' schedules.

ABOVE: The Courtyard by Marriott's outdoor swimming pool area is lined with chairs and chaise lounges and has a gazebo nearby that offers a break from the sun.

RIGHT: The hotel's lounge—with its fireplace and comfortable furnishings—offers a quiet place to relax and unwind.

LEFT: *Located just seconds from the intersection of Interstates 430 and 630, the Courtyard by Marriott is convenient to travelers coming from or working in any direction.*

BELOW: *All of the Courtyard by Marriott's guest rooms include a seating area.*

There is a laundry room with washers and dryers, or guests can take advantage of the Courtyard's dry-cleaning service, which picks up and delivers laundry daily.

The Courtyard's restaurant offers guests a variety of breakfast choices. A buffet provides a range of traditional favorites such as eggs, bacon, sausage, and biscuits and gravy as well as lighter choices such as cereal, fresh fruit, and bagels. Diners also can order from the Courtyard's extensive menu. The hotel's lounge is open from 4 p.m. to midnight Monday through Friday, and—with its fireplace and comfortable furnishings—offers a quiet place to relax and unwind.

RAPIDLY GROWING CHAIN

Marriott International founded its chain of Courtyard hotels in 1983 in Atlanta. The Little Rock hotel is a corporate-owned property, though many of the Courtyards are franchise operations. The company expects more than 300 Courtyard hotels by the end of 1996, with 700 planned by 2000. The chain has an 83 percent average occupancy rate nationwide, and the Little Rock hotel often exceeds that figure, primarily thanks to its many repeat customers.

For those business travelers who spend many nights a year on the road, Courtyard by Marriott has established its Courtyard Club, a frequent-visitor organization that offers several incentives. After 12 nights, Courtyard Club members get one night free or may choose instead to have 1,750 frequent-flier miles added to their accounts with either American, USAir, or Delta Airlines. Repeat guests also get 10 percent off the already lower weekend rate. Club members receive free local telephone calls when they stay at Courtyard, free fax service, and a special toll-free number to make reservations.

To speed the reservation process, Courtyard Club members fill out a card in advance that lists room preferences such as bed size, and smoking or nonsmoking rooms. Club members simply call for a reservation, pick up the key at check-in, and leave the rest of the paperwork to Courtyard staff. Courtyard Club Gold members, who achieve that status by staying at Courtyard at least 36 nights in one year, are eligible for even more amenities.

Courtyard's commitment to the business traveler extends to the ultimate detail of all—the beds in

each guest room. Jameson, a leading name in bedding manufacturing, custom-makes each bed at Courtyard by Marriott. The beds are replaced every few years as part of each Courtyard location's complete makeover.

To keep its appearance appealing to guests, the Courtyard undergoes frequent renovations that include new furniture and carpets, and a fresh coat of paint. Little Rock's Courtyard by Marriott was completely remodeled near the end of 1994, with another full refurbishing scheduled for 1998—gearing up to serve the Little Rock area for years to come.

AT&T Wireless Services, Inc.

THE LEADING PROVIDER OF CELLULAR SERVICES IN THE UNITED STATES, AT&T WIRELESS SERVICES, INC. COVERS 80 PERCENT OF THE U.S. POPULATION AND IS IN 25 OF THE TOP 27 U.S. MARKETS. MORE THAN 5.5 MILLION CUSTOMERS IN 105 LICENSED SERVICE AREAS ARE LINKED THROUGH THE COMPANY'S NORTH AMERICAN CELLULAR NETWORK. ❧ THE COMPANY ALSO IS THE LEADING

cellular provider in Arkansas, covering more than 95 percent of the state. As the state's largest cellular service company, AT&T Wireless Services offers special airtime rate plans, including one that permits customers who travel across Arkansas to pay low hometown rates whenever they are making calls in an AT&T service area. Customers in Arkansas also are connected to more than 5,000 cities in North America and many other countries through the vast North American Cellular Network.

AT&T entered the wireless communication service business in a major way, acquiring McCaw Cellular Communications, the firm credited with creating the cellular industry. McCaw operated in Arkansas under the brand name of Cellular One. In the fall of 1995 Cellular One converted to the AT&T wireless services brand.

Because of its strong position as an established cellular service firm in Arkansas, AT&T Wireless Services is making sure Arkansas remains in the forefront in the development and deployment of wireless cellular technology for personal and business applications.

Customers in Arkansas are served by 169 authorized dealers and seven AT&T Wireless Services customer convenience centers in Little Rock, El Dorado, Fort Smith, Fayetteville, Jonesboro, Russellville, and Searcy. A free call to a 24-hour-a-day Customer Care Center also provides immediate access to representatives who can provide help and answer questions.

THE FUTURE

AT&T Wireless Services walked away from 1995's Federal Communications Commission (FCC) auc-

ranging new advanced services including Caller ID, message waiting indicator for voice mail, short messaging service on cellular phones, longer battery life, privacy, and additional voice and data services.

tion as one of the big winners. The company invested $1.7 billion to purchase 21 new licensed areas. The new licenses were auctioned under the name of personal communication services (PCS). The government made available the new licenses to accommodate the massive growth projected in the cellular business over the next few years.

To achieve its goal of building a seamless, advanced nationwide wireless communications system, AT&T will deploy the latest digital technology in both its established markets such as Arkansas and its newly acquired PCS markets such as St. Louis and Atlanta. The company views PCS as an extension to existing cellular technology, not as a replacement.

AT&T Wireless Services is a wholly owned subsidiary of AT&T and is the leading provider of wireless communications services in the United States, including cellular telephone, messaging, wireless data transmission, air-to-ground and ground-to-air phone, and satellite.

RIGHT: AT&T Wireless Services, Inc. is the leading cellular provider in Arkansas, covering more than 95 percent of the state.

BELOW: Customers in Arkansas are connected to more than 5,000 cities in North America and many other countries through the vast North American Cellular Network.

BELOW RIGHT: The next generation of digital cellular technology will be deployed by AT&T throughout Arkansas, enabling cellular customers access to wide-ranging new advanced services.

INVESTING IN ARKANSAS

In Arkansas alone, AT&T Wireless Services has invested since 1994 more than $75 million to build a world-class wireless network. The next generation of digital cellular technology will be deployed throughout Arkansas, enabling cellular customers access to wide-

PHOTOGRAPHERS

WILLIE ALLEN has been a self-employed professional photographer for 35 years, specializing in advertising, photojournalism, and film and video production. He has worked for the *Arkansas Gazette*, covering the integration of Central High School, and United Press International in Los Angeles, photographing the Democratic Convention. Allen's coverage of numerous major news and sports stories throughout Mississippi, Louisiana, and Texas can be seen in *Time*, *Newsweek*, and *Money* magazines as well as in newspapers around the world. His clients include such major corporations as AT&T, Exxon, Fairfield Communities, International Paper, and United Airlines.

WESLEY HITT, a native of North Little Rock, is a graduate of the Hallmark Institute of Photography in Massachusetts. Specializing in stock, people, and corporate photography, he is the recipient of a Gold Addy for the 1995 Dillard's annual report. Two of Hitt's photographs are top sellers for Liaison International Stock Agency.

JAN WILSON JOROLAN, formerly of Dallas, is a nature and international travel photographer who lives in Hot Springs, Arkansas. Her travels have taken her through much of the United States and to such exotic places as the mountain cloud forest of Mexico, Central and South America, Europe, Russia, Turkey, and central and southern Africa. Jorolan is a member of the Photographic Society of America, Nikon Professional Services, International Network of Publishing Photographers, and several environmental organizations and committees. Her work has been published in various travel and other publications and has won regional, state, and international honors.

DIXIE KNIGHT, the owner and operator of Dixie Knight Photography, specializes in black-and-white portraiture. Originally from Napa, California, she moved to Little Rock in 1975. Knight has photographically illustrated three books: *Zap! Ray Gun Classics*, *Legacy in Clay: The Ceramic Art of Pre-Historic Arkansas*, and *Embossed American Axes*.

BRETT LILE, who was born and raised in Little Rock, brings 35 years of experience to his chosen career of photography. The owner of Lile Photographic, Inc., he specializes in commercial, advertising, industrial, and aerial photography. Lile's previous clients include such major corporations as AT&T, Disney, Southwestern Bell, United Technologies, Atlantic Research, Gilbert Central Construction, Jennings Osborne, and Arkansas Research Medical.

BUDDY MAYS, from Bend, Oregon, is a leading stock and assignment photographer who has visited and photographed more than 60 countries. He has authored and illustrated more than a dozen books on travel, archaeology, and wildlife, including *A Berlitz Traveller's Guide to the American Southwest* and *A Berlitz Traveller's Guide to Costa Rica*. Mays' color images appear regularly in such publications as the *New York Times*, *Audubon*, *Forbes*, *Natural History*, *Sierra*, *Endless Vacation*, the *Los Angeles Times*, *Newsday*, *Vista USA*, *Odyssey*, and *Better Homes and*

Gardens. Among Mays' numerous awards in national and international photography competition are Best Portfolio from the Society of American Travel Writers and runner-up for the coveted Lowell Thomas award for color photography. He was also nominated for a Pulitzer Prize in feature photography for his work on American cowboys.

BILL PARSONS, a graduate of the University of Arkansas in Fayetteville, has been in business in Little Rock for 25 years. Specializing in advertising and corporate photography, he is a widely published photographer who devotes his spare time to fine art and travel photography.

PAGES 139 AND 142: WESLEY HITT

PAGES 140 AND 144: MATT BRADLEY

INDEX OF PROFILES